A GOURMET'S BOOK OF

VEGETABLES

LOUISE STEELE

Photographed by
DAVID GILL

a Salamander book

Published by Salamander Books Limited
LONDON • NEW YORK

Published 1989 by Salamander Books Ltd,
52 Bedford Row, London, WC1R 4LR

This book was created by Merehurst Limited
Ferry House, 51/57 Lacy Road, Putney, London, SW15 1PR

© 1989 Salamander Books Ltd

ISBN : 0 86101 404 9

Distributed by Hodder and Stoughton Services,
PO Box 6, Mill Road, Dunton Green,
Sevenoaks, Kent TN13 2XX

Commissioned and Directed by Merehurst Limited
Managing Editor : Janet Illsley
Photographer : David Gill
Designer : Sue Storey
Editor : Maureen Callis
Home Economist : Maxine Clark
Assistant Home Ecomonist : Jacqueline Clark
Stylist : Maria Kelly
Typeset by Walkergate Press Ltd, Anlaby, Hull
Colour reproduction by Kentscan, England
Printed in Belgium by Proost International Book Production, Turnhout

COMPANION VOLUMES OF INTEREST:
A Gourmet's Book of FRUIT
A Gourmet's Book of HERBS & SPICES
A Gourmet's Book of CHEESE
A Gourmet's Book of CHOCOLATE
A Gourmet's Book of TEA & COFFEE

Contents

Notes for Recipe Users
Quantities are given in metric, imperial and Australian cups.
Use one set of measures only: they are not interchangeable.

All spoon measures are level: 1 tablespoon = 15 ml spoon;
1 teaspoon = 5 ml spoon.

Use fresh herbs unless otherwise stated.

Australian users, note spring onions are the variety commonly termed
'green shallot' or simply 'shallot' in Australia. Where a recipe
specifies shallot, use a 'brown shallot'.

Introduction

Try to imagine a world without vegetables – it's a bleak thought! Fortunately, instead, we are almost spoilt for choice with a glorious range of delicious vegetables. Never before has such a variety been available in supermarkets and specialist greengrocers.

Vegetables come in a dazzling array of colours and shapes, with wonderful flavours and textures – some more familiar to us than others. A Gourmet's Book of Vegetables aims to help you make the most of them, with practical advice on when to buy and what to look for, plus plenty of information on preparation and cooking, imaginative serving suggestions, and a feast of beautifully illustrated step-by-step recipes.

The vegetables have been grouped according to type: brassicas, root vegetables, onions, peas and beans, stalks and stems, fruiting vegetables and so on. Each section is illustrated with colour photographs to make the less familiar ones easy to identify.

The recipe section includes ideas for soups and starters, main courses, accompaniments and salads, plus a selection of vegetarian main courses. Some ideas will, hopefully, inspire you – some may even surprise you! Suggestions range from Spiced Pumpkin Soup and Wafer-Wrapped Vegetables to Sorrel & Asparagus Crêpes and Cucumber & Strawberry Salad.

Whether you would like to experiment with unfamiliar vegetables or simply add to your own repertoire of vegetable dishes, you will surely find plenty of ideas here to grace any table and delight the gourmet palate.

Cabbage

The cabbage (*Brassica oleracea var. capitata*) is said to have originated in the eastern Mediterranean and Asia Minor. This indispensable, though much maligned, vegetable has changed a lot through the centuries and it was not until the 16th century that the firm-headed types appeared.

There are many different varieties available throughout the year: green, white and red. They may be round or conical, tightly-packed or loose-leaved, smooth or curly. Green cabbages are the most widely grown and are around all year.

Spring cabbage, in season from winter through to spring, is a young cabbage harvested when the heart is only partially developed. It has smooth dark green leaves, which are loose or small-hearted.

Spring greens are small, young, mid-green leafy cabbages, sold before the hearts have developed.

Savoy cabbage – considered to be one of the best for flavour – is the pretty one with crisp, curling outer leaves and a firm green head. It is available from late summer.

White cabbage has a firm, hard, crisp head with smooth leaves and is available for most of the year.

Red cabbage is in season from spring until mid-winter. It is hard, tightly-packed, crisp and – as the name suggests – dark red or crimson.

Bok choy from China, also known as Chinese cabbage or Chinese chard, is a slender type of cabbage with broad green leaves, tapering to crisp white stalks. It is similar in appearance to Swiss chard and should not be confused with Chinese leaves, which are white and crisp (see page 12). It is available from Chinese supermarkets and some specialist greengrocers. It is usually served stir-fried, although it may be prepared and served in the same way as other types of cabbage.

Buying and Storing
Choose fresh-looking cabbages with compact heads. A good quality cabbage should weigh heavy in the hand. It is best to use cabbage as soon as possible after buying or harvesting, although the hard varieties keep well for a week or more in a cool place. Store the more leafy varieties in a polythene bag in the salad drawer of the refrigerator for up to 2 days.

Preparation and Cooking
Discard coarse outer leaves and wash the cabbage thoroughly. Cut hard types into halves or quarters for easy handling. Cut away the centre stalk, then shred, cut into wedges or leave whole, depending on how the cabbage is to be used.

Cabbage is all too often ruined by overcooking: it should be cooked only until tender-crisp to enjoy its flavour and texture; over-cooking also deprives this vegetable of its nutritional content. Steam or boil in a very small amount of salted water or chicken stock until just tender: 5-7 minutes for shredded cabbage; about 12 minutes for wedges or quarters. Always drain well before serving.

Serving Suggestions
The hard red and white types are delicious shredded raw into salads: try a mixture of the two with beansprouts and green pepper, dressed in a ginger vinaigrette.

Red cabbage is most often used either in pickling or for long, slow cooking in braises and casseroles; it is excellent with rich meats such as venison, duckling and sausages.

The hard white type, cut in wedges, makes a lovely addition to casseroles or pot roasts and chunky soups in the French style.

Use blanched cabbage leaves (Savoy are perfect) to enclose meat and rice fillings for tasty variations on the Greek Dolmades theme.

Try cabbage Chinese-style: stir-fried it retains its colour and crispness. Bok choy is particularly good cooked this way: coarsely shred the leaves and stalks crosswise before stir-frying. Cook well-dried finely shredded spring greens oriental-style: deep-fry until crisp and use as 'seaweed' in Chinese dishes.

Savoy cabbage

Spring cabbage

Miniature red cabbage

Red cabbage

Spring greens

White cabbage

Brussels sprout

Brussels Sprout

Brussels sprouts (*Brassica oleracea var. bullata gemmifera*) were first grown in Brussels as long ago as the 13th century. However, it was not until the early 19th century that they arrived in Britain.

These vegetables, like miniature, tight-headed cabbages, belong to the Brassica family and are in season during autumn and winter. Their flavour is said to be improved by a touch of frost.

Buying and Storing
Look for small, firm, fresh green sprouts. They will keep well for up to 2 days, stored loosely in a polythene bag in the salad drawer of the refrigerator.

Preparation and Cooking
Wash just before cooking, remove any loose outer leaves, trim stem end (not too close or sprouts will fall apart during cooking), then cut a cross in the base of the stalk to help even cooking.

Do take care when cooking – sprouts really are most unpleasant if overcooked (as they all too often are!). Bring a pan of salted water to the boil, add sprouts, cover and cook at a full, rolling boil for 6-8 minutes (depending on size), until only just tender and still bright green in colour. They may also be steamed (in which case allow a few extra minutes cooking time), or braised in a little butter and chicken stock. Drain Brussels sprouts well before serving.

Serving Suggestions
When at their peak, young and tender sprouts are delicious finely shredded and served raw in winter salads or added to stir-fry dishes. Brussels sprouts with chestnuts are traditionally served with the Christmas turkey, and are a good accompaniment at other times; use canned chestnuts when fresh are unavailable.

Sprouts are also delicious served tossed in melted butter with a sprinkling of crisp, crumbled bacon and tiny garlic croûtons. Sprouts puréed with butter, cream, mashed potato and a little nutmeg make a dish that's both colourful and tasty; or try them puréed in a cream soup, garnished with dainty fleurons of puff pastry and a sprinkling of Emmenthal cheese.

Kohl-rabi

Despite its rather strange appearance, Kohl-rabi (*Brassica oleracea caulorapa var. gaugyloides*) is a member of the cabbage family. It is believed to have originated in the East and is particularly popular in European countries and the Orient. It has a round swollen green or purple stem base, from which leaf stems grow.

Buying and Storing
Kohl-rabi is available from summer until early winter. Select firm small bulbs, ideally no larger than a tennis ball – any bigger and they tend to be coarse-textured. They will keep in the salad drawer of the refrigerator for up to 3 days.

Preparation and Cooking
Trim off stalk ends, peel thinly, then quarter or slice (according to size and recipe). Cook, covered, in boiling salted water for 20-25 minutes, until tender; allow a few minutes longer if steaming. Kohl-rabi may also be cooked then peeled, if preferred.

Serving Suggestions
Small kohl-rabi can be eaten raw. It is delicious peeled and grated or chopped into salads – the crisp texture and sweet, delicate flavour (similar to that of a young turnip) add 'bite' and interest. Or coat the grated vegetable in a lightly curried mayonnaise and spoon into crisp lettuce cups to serve as an original first course.

Add diced raw kohl-rabi to casseroles, stocks and soups or use as you would turnip and swede. Try it cooked and tossed in melted butter, hollandaise or a cream sauce; or coated with béchamel, sprinkled with cheese and flashed under the grill until golden. Stuffed kohl-rabi is also excellent: hollow out vegetable, fill with a tasty meat stuffing and poach in stock until tender.

Kohl-rabi

Cauliflower

The cauliflower (*Brassica oleracea var. botrytis cauliflora*) originated in the Mediterranean region and first appeared in England and France around the end of the 16th century.

Both summer and winter varieties are available throughout the year. On summer cauliflowers the leaves are opened out around the head (known as curds), but on winter types the leaves are folded over the head. Green flowering varieties are available too.

Buying and Storing
Size does not denote quality. Choose cauliflowers with creamy white (or green), firm and compact heads. Do not buy those where the white flower heads are beginning to open. If not using immediately, store, loosely wrapped in a polythene bag, in the salad drawer of the refrigerator for up to 2 days.

Preparation and Cooking
To cook whole, cut off all but the smallest, tender inner leaves, wash thoroughly and make a deep cross in the base of the stalk. Cook, covered, in the minimum of boiling salted water for 12-15 minutes, so that it steam-cooks (the stem in the boiling water and the head in the steam) until just tender. To cook flowerets, break or cut into even pieces and cook for 5-6 minutes. Cauliflower, whole or flowerets, may also be steamed (sprinkled with lemon juice), if preferred; allow a few minutes extra cooking time.

Serving Suggestions
Use small flowerets and small slices of crunchy stalk raw in salads, or with dips. They are also good parcooked and tossed (still warm) in vinaigrette and served chilled with red kidney beans and flaked tuna or peeled prawns as a first course.

Hot cauliflower is delicious drizzled with browned butter and a sprinkling of fresh herbs, or coated with a rich white or cheese sauce. Or cook it whole Polonaise-style, garnished with butter-crisp breadcrumbs, parsley, sieved egg yolk and finely chopped egg white. Try cauliflower flowerets, braised in butter and a little stock spiced with mace, as an accompaniment. Cauliflower also makes a tasty soup.

Chinese Leaf

Chinese leaves (*Brassica pekinensis*) are also known as *napa* cabbage, celery cabbage or *pe-tsai* – and sometimes, incorrectly, as Chinese cabbage (see page 8). Although this is a relatively new vegetable to Western countries, it has been known in China and parts of Asia since the 5th century.

Chinese leaves look rather like a cross between a head of celery and a Cos lettuce – being long, slender and tightly-packed with pale green leaves on the edges of thick, white, crisp rib-stems.

Buying and Preparation
Chinese leaves are available throughout the year. They can be quite large, so are often sold in halves. Choose only firm, crisp heads and store for up to 1 week in the salad drawer of the refrigerator. To prepare, trim off base, rinse in cold water, then pat dry. Chop, slice, shred or separate into stems.

Serving Suggestions
This deliciously crisp and juicy vegetable is good to eat both raw and cooked. It is used extensively in Chinese dishes.

The tender inner leaves are lovely shredded raw into salads and coleslaws. Serve the stems cut into sticks with cheese and crusty bread.

Try the outer leaves sliced and stir-fried in a little garlic-flavoured oil until tender-crisp, or shred and add to soups.

The juicy stems make succulent eating: trim off green leafy parts and either braise stems with butter and onions, or simmer until just tender and serve tossed in melted butter or cream and herbs.

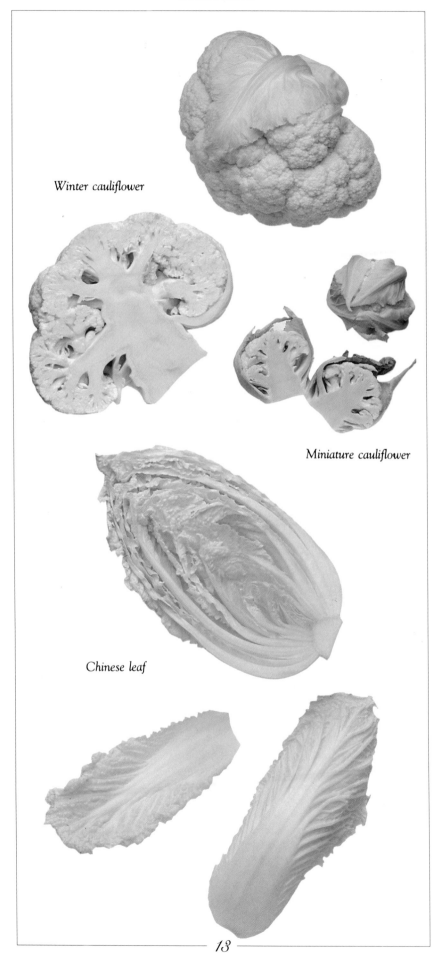

Winter cauliflower

Miniature cauliflower

Chinese leaf

Broccoli

Broccoli (*Brassica oleracea var. italica*) is a member of the Brassica family. It originally came from Asia Minor and the Mediterranean region, and was first cultivated in Italy in the 16th century. The small purple sprouting type, with small clusters of purple flowers sprouting up the stem, is widely known in northern Europe. White and green varieties are also available. Calabrese or 'Italian broccoli' has larger flower heads on the stems. It is imported from Italy, and is also grown commercially in Britain. Broccoli and calabrese are completely interchangeable and are cooked and eaten in the same way.

Broccoli is available virtually all year round and calabrese from midsummer through to early winter.

Buying and Storing
Choose broccoli and calabrese with tight compact heads and firm stalks which snap easily. Both types store well, wrapped loosely in polythene bags, in the salad drawer of the refrigerator for up to 3 days.

Preparation and Cooking
Trim off tough lower part of stems and divide thicker stalks in half to ensure even cooking. Cook them covered, in a very little boiling salted water for 5-10 minutes (or steam for 10-12 minutes) until tender-crisp. To prevent overcooking the more tender flower heads, tie broccoli spears together in bundles and stand upright in a small pan, so that stalks boil while the flower heads only steam.

Broccoli is good stir-fried: divide flower heads and slice stalks.

Serving Suggestions
Tender, young broccoli and calabrese spears are good cut up and eaten raw in salads – or par-cooked until nutty crisp, if preferred. Cooked this way they also make excellent 'dunking' sticks for dips and fondues. Blanched spears, wrapped in puff pastry and baked, or dipped in a light batter and fried, are perfect served with a tasty dip.

Broccoli is delicious served with a sauce, such as brown butter with capers or toasted flaked almonds, or covered with a tangy cheese and herb sauce, sprinkled with buttered crumbs and baked. A mixture of broccoli and cauliflower flowerets, par-cooked, then stir-fried in a spicy butter (see page 107) makes a good accompaniment. Puréed broccoli makes an excellent soup.

Kale

Kale (*Brassica oleracea var. acephala*) is native to the eastern Mediterranean and Asia Minor. It is also known as curly kale or borecole (collards in America). A cabbage without a solid head (or heart), it can be flat or curly with heavily crimped leaves and prominent mid-ribs, and varies in colour from dark green to purple. Kale has coarse-textured leaves and a stronger flavour than other cabbages.

Buying and Storing
Kale is in season during winter and spring. Choose fresh looking plants, avoiding any that are wilted or yellowing. Kale will keep for 2-3 days in a polythene bag in the salad drawer of the refrigerator.

Preparation and Cooking
Cut off root end, strip leaves from stalks and tear into 2 or 3 pieces, or shred coarsely. Cover and cook in boiling salted water (or braise with a little stock and butter) for about 10 minutes, until tender; or steam for 12-15 minutes; drain thoroughly before serving.

Serving Suggestions
Kale has a rather pronounced flavour and for this reason is best served on its own as an accompaniment. Serve it simply tossed in melted butter and plenty of black pepper, or drizzled with cream, snipped chives and crisp slivers of fried bacon. It is also good served with béchamel sauce.

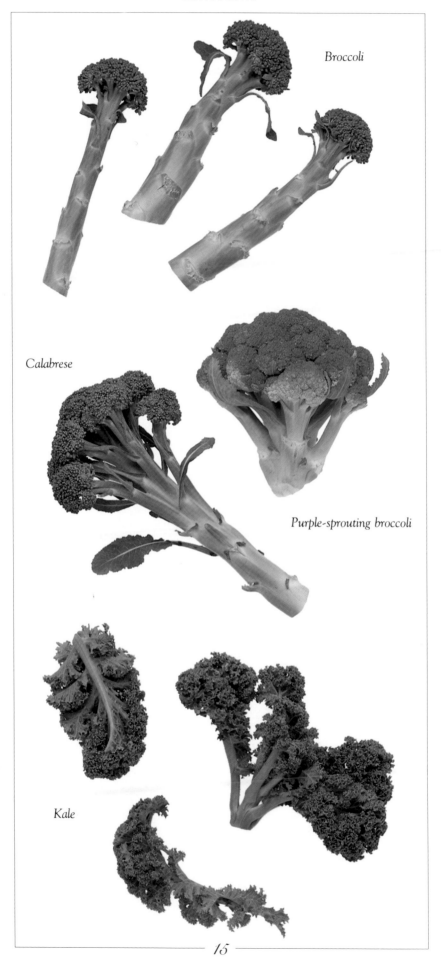

Broccoli

Calabrese

Purple-sprouting broccoli

Kale

Lettuce

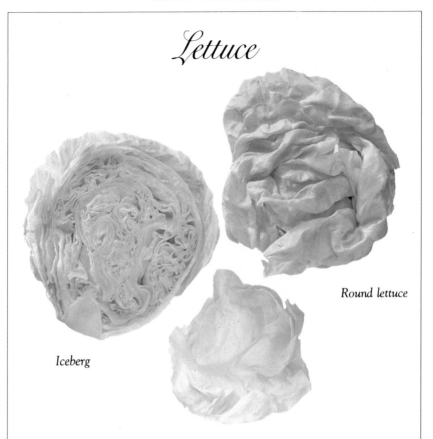

Round lettuce

Iceberg

The lettuce (*Lactuca sativa*) was cultivated in Britain in the 15th century, more likely for cooking than eating raw. Suggestions as to its origins range from the Mediterranean to Siberia!

Lettuces come in many shapes and sizes, but there are three main groups: the cabbage or butterhead type, the Cos (or Romaine) lettuce, and the loose-leaf lettuce.

Cabbage lettuces have round heads and range from the soft round lettuce to the crisp delicious Webb's Wonderful, the crunchy, tight-hearted Icebergs and the dwarf hearty Little Gem with its sweet flavour.

The Cos lettuce is a crisp, flavoursome, long-leaved lettuce. A red-leaved Cos is now available.

Loose-leaf lettuce varieties include the curly light green leaved Salad Bowl, the red oak-leaf type (also called *Feuille de Chêne*) and Lollo Rosso, a frilly red-edged lettuce with a slightly bitter flavour.

Celtuce is a lesser known non-heading variety, with stiff green leaves on a stem, which is also eaten. It is often called asparagus lettuce, as its flavour is a cross between asparagus and lettuce.

Buying and Storing
Lettuces are available all year and there will generally be several varieties to choose from. Whichever you buy it should be fresh with a good colour. Lettuce is best eaten fresh, although most types will keep in the salad drawer of the refrigerator for up to 2 days.

Preparation
Trim base of lettuce and remove any tough outer leaves, then wash and dry before using. It is better to tear lettuce with your hands, as cutting it with a knife causes bruising and discolouring; if shredded lettuce is required, do this at the last moment.

Serving Suggestions
Lettuce is mainly used in salads, ranging from simple green salads to the more elaborate Caesar, Waldorf and Niçoise. It is also very tasty cooked: stir-fried shredded lettuce is extremely good – or try lettuce hearts braised in butter and stock (or wine) and served drizzled with cream and chopped herbs. Lettuce and sorrel soup is quite delicious – serve chilled, topped with thick sour cream.

Webb's wonderful

Lollo rosso

Oak-leaf lettuce

Little gem

Cos lettuce

Endive

Endive (*Cichorium endivia*) has been cultivated in Europe since around the end of the 13th century. It is related to chicory and is known as *chicorée frisée* in France and, sometimes, as chicory in America.

There are two basic types: curly endive has narrow curly leaves, with dark green outer leaves and very pale inner ones; the Batavian endive (often called Batavia or escarole) is broader-leaved and less curly. Some Batavian endive are tightly-packed and have a blue-green tinge, others are looser-leaved. Both types of endive are bitter-flavoured, although the Batavian type is less so.

Curly endive is in the shops all year round – choose one with a nice light centre as the darker the leaves the more bitter the flavour. Batavian endive is less widely available, but is becoming more so.

Both types are best eaten freshly purchased, but can be stored briefly in a polythene bag in the salad drawer of the refrigerator.

Serving Suggestions
Once washed, trimmed and dried, the leaves are included in salads and salad-based hors d'oeuvres, when they are excellent dressed in a good, stong vinaigrette to complement their bitter flavour. Curly endive looks especially attractive used on open sandwiches and as a garnish. The leaves are also delicious lightly sautéed in butter.

Chicory

Chicory (*Cichorium intybus*) was developed from the wild plant succory, a native of Europe. White chicory, the most familiar type, is also known as Belgian endive, sometimes simply endive in France, and witloof in Belgium.

White chicory is produced by cutting off the natural foliage and forcing the roots (in the dark) to yield long, white, tightly-packed heads of leaves (or white chicons).

Available from autumn to spring; look for conical, crisp, white, tightly-packed heads, avoiding any with green tips – these will be bitter. Chicory is best eaten fresh, but can be kept wrapped in dark paper, to preserve the white colour, in the refrigerator for 2-3 days.

Preparation and Cooking
Cut off root base, remove any damaged outer leaves and wash. Leave whole, divide into leaves or slice, as required. To cook whole chicory heads, blanch in boiling water, with lemon juice added, for 4-5 minutes, or steam for 6-7 minutes. Or braise in butter and stock.

Serving Suggestions
Raw chicory is a delicious addition to salads; it goes particularly well with citrus fruits and nuts. Par-cooked chicory, wrapped in ham, coated with cheese sauce and baked *au gratin* is good. Or try it braised in butter and wine with shallots and tomatoes, or steamed and tossed in melted butter or cream and herbs.

Radicchio

Radicchio (*Cichorium intybus var. foliosum*), or red chicory, originated in Italy. It is closely related to endive. There are several types: forced radicchio resembles chicory in shape and size, and has a white head with dark red-edged leaves; Rossa de Treviso is more open with dark red oblong leaves and creamy-white stalks; Rossa di Verona is round, like a small, tight lettuce head, with cerise leaves and white stalks and veins. All types are similar in flavour to chicory.

This vegetable has become increasingly popular for its attractive colour, in salads and hors d'oeuvres. It is served raw or cooked in the same way as chicory (see above).

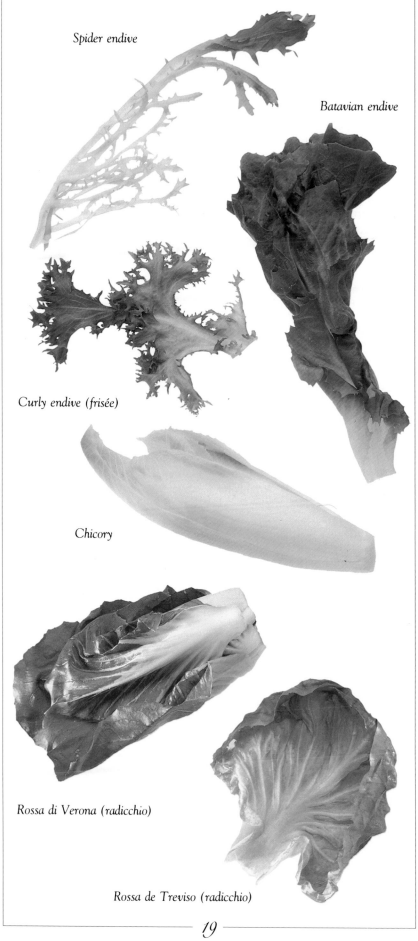

Spider endive

Batavian endive

Curly endive (frisée)

Chicory

Rossa di Verona (radicchio)

Rossa de Treviso (radicchio)

Spinach

Spinach (*Spinacia oleracea*) has vague origins: some say it originated in Persia, others that it is native to the Far East. It was certainly eaten by the Greeks and Romans and arrived in northern Europe during the 16th century.

There are two types of true spinach: a summer variety and a winter spinach, making it available throughout the year. True spinach or 'English spinach' has a more delicate flavour than other types.

Spinach Beet (*Beta vulgaris* var. *cicla*), also called perpetual spinach, is coarser in texture – but grows happily all year round, even in the coldest weather. It makes a good substitute when true spinach is unavailable. If you've a patch of soil to spare, this is a good vegetable to grow: keep picking the leaves throughout the year to ensure a constant supply of new, young, tender ones.

New Zealand spinach (*Tetragonia expansa)* is not spinach at all, but it does come from New Zealand! It never gained the popularity in Britain that it did in Europe and the United States. It has a mild, sweet flavour with smaller, tougher leaves than true spinach.

Good King Henry (*Chenopodium bonus-henricus*), also known as mercury or wild spinach, is native to Britain. It may be substituted for true spinach in cooking.

Buying and Storing

Spinach wilts quickly, so buy as fresh as possible and use quickly. If using for cooking, rather than salads, store in the refrigerator in a polythene bag for up to 2 days.

Preparation and Cooking

Spinach must be washed thoroughly in several changes of cold water as the slightest speck of grit or sand will ruin the finished dish. Discard tough centre stalks. Shake off excess moisture and pack spinach into a large saucepan. Do not add any water – the moisture clinging to the leaves is sufficient for cooking. Cover tightly and heat gently, turning occasionally until spinach decreases in volume; bring to the boil and cook for 8-10 minutes, until tender. Drain well in a colander or sieve, pressing spinach firmly against the side using a saucer to force out all moisture.

Serving Suggestions

When young and tender (and very fresh), spinach leaves in a good dressing make an excellent salad – on their own or with a selection of mixed salad leaves and other ingredients (see page 114).

Spinach leaves may be shredded and stirred into Chinese soups and are delicious stir-fried briefly with flavourings, such as fresh root (green) ginger, garlic and chillies.

Cooked, puréed or chopped spinach forms a splendid basis for soups, soufflés and crêpe fillings and, mixed with cream, eggs and cheese, makes a delicious quiche.

To serve as an accompaniment, toss cooked spinach in melted butter, seasonings and a pinch of grated nutmeg. For a richer dish, mix with double (thick) cream and chopped herbs, or coat spinach with béchamel, sprinkle with Emmenthal cheese and flash under a hot grill until golden.

Sorrel

Sorrel (*Rumex acetosa*) grows wild in most European regions. Of the two main varieties available, the French type is considered better for cooking, as it has a mild flavour. Sorrel is actually a herb which is served as a vegetable, in similar ways to spinach (see above).

The succulent leaves, shaped like elongated arrow heads, are green and glossy with a slightly acid, sharp flavour. They are highly-prized in France and used in a variety of dishes.

Buying and Storing

Sorrel is not widely available in shops, although you may find that

Spinach beet

English spinach

French sorrel

specialist greengrocers stock it during the summer. It is best eaten fresh, though it can be stored in a polythene bag in the refrigerator for 2 to 3 days.

If growing your own sorrel – and it is well worth doing so, either from seed or buy a small pot from your local garden centre – pick the leaves when young and small (this also encourages the plant to produce more leaves) as they become very bitter if left to grow large.

Preparation and Cooking
Pick off and discard stems. Wash leaves well and shake dry. Cook as for spinach (opposite) for a few minutes until tender, or sauté in a little butter over a low heat until wilted and tender. Chop or purée and use as required.

Serving Suggestions
Sorrel is a wonderful addition to green salads and is also good chopped and added to omelettes. A few leaves added to fish before baking impart an excellent flavour. Puréed sorrel, mixed with cream and stock, makes a favourite soup; or use the purée for soufflés, or as an unusual base for Eggs Florentine, instead of spinach. Puréed sorrel is also a perfect accompaniment to veal and fish dishes.

Watercress

Watercress (*Nasturtium officinale*) is an aquatic plant that grows wild in freshwater streams throughout Europe. It is also widely cultivated in 'watercress beds' in several countries.

Buying and Storing
Watercress is available all year, sold in bunches or ready-trimmed in vacuum packs. Choose watercress with dark green, glossy leaves. Un-opened packs keep in the refrigerator for up to 3 days; bunches should be kept in a polythene bag in the refrigerator and used within 1 day. To liven up watercress, put bunches (leaves down) in a bowl of cold water for several hours. Wash well and trim stalks before using.

Serving Suggestions
Watercress makes an excellent garnish and is splendid in salads – try it with segments of orange and chicory, tossed in a walnut oil dressing.

Mixed with shredded radicchio it makes a colourful and unusual base for prawn cocktails. Use the finely chopped leaves to flavour (and colour) butters and dips, and to make stuffings – especially good for lamb or fish. Add whole leaves to omelettes, quiches and stir-fry dishes.

Serve a watercress sauce with fish or veal, and watercress mayonnaise with cold salmon. Watercress soup is delicious, served hot or cold.

AMERICAN CRESS AND WINTER CRESS
American cress (*Barbarea praecox*), or land cress as it is also known, is native to America. Winter cress (*Barbarea vulgaris*) from Europe is closely related. These are both similar in flavour to watercress and far easier to grow at home in a shady, damp corner of the garden. Prepare and use both of these varieties as you would watercress.

Winter cress

Watercress

Corn salad

Salad cress

Salad Cress

Salad cress (*Lepidium sativum*) is sometimes incorrectly called mustard and cress. At one time cress was grown from a mixture of pepper cress seeds and mustard seeds; however, nowadays most commercially grown cress is produced from rape seeds only.

Salad cress is available all year round and is sold in small punnets, still growing. These punnets keep fresh for up to 3 days stored in a polythene bag in the salad drawer of the refrigerator.

To use, simply snip off cress, wash thoroughly and pat dry. Use in salads and sandwich fillings (it is especially good with egg and cream cheese mixtures) or as a dainty garnish. Salad cress also makes a crisp and interesting omelette or savoury crêpe filling, mixed with crispy fried bacon pieces and grated cheese.

Corn Salad

Corn salad (*Valerianella locusto*), also known as lamb's lettuce and as *mâche* in France, has been cultivated from the wild variety which grows in cornfields. The plant has small, soft green leaves (the shape of lamb's tongues) with a velvety texture and a delicate flavour.

Look for corn salad in specialist greengrocers and supermarkets throughout the year. It is a hardy plant to grow at home and makes a good winter substitute for lettuce.

Wash, pat dry and use with other leaves in salads or as a decorative border for mousses and pâtés. It is also good lightly sautéed in butter as an accompaniment.

Dandelion

The dandelion (*Taraxacum officinale*) is believed to be one of the 'bitter herbs' mentioned in the Old Testament. Although generally regarded as a most persistent weed in Britain, various strains of dandelion plant are cultivated in Europe. The cultivated types are larger than the wild dandelion, tightly-packed with dark green leaves and white stems.

Cultivated dandelions are sometimes available from specialist greengrocers during the summer. The wild type should be picked in early spring while young and tender; pick away from roadsides where they may have been chemically sprayed. Wash dandelions very thoroughly before use.

Serving Suggestions
The leaves have a slightly bitter flavour which is good in salads; sprinkle the flower petals on top for a pretty effect. Or use them in the classic French salad *Salade de Pissenlits au Lard*: a combination of dandelion leaves, crisp fried bacon pieces and croûtons, dressed in a vinaigrette, with the hot bacon fat poured over before serving. Or add shredded leaves to stir-fry dishes.

The roots are used, dried and ground, to make a coffee substitute which is sold in health-food shops.

Nettle

The stinging nettle (*Urtica dioica*) is one of the most common edible wild plants, growing abundantly in almost any environment. At one time nettle beds were a feature in English gardens – the nettles being prized for their nutritional quality.

Nettles are around in spring and summer. Of course, you won't find them in the shops – what you must do is don a pair of rubber gloves and go foraging! Incidentally, once cooked the sting is destroyed!

Nettles are extremely good when young. The best time to pick them is when the tender shoots are still short, or just pluck off the tops and pale green leaves of more mature plants (the darker leaves are coarse and unpleasantly bitter). Avoid those near roadsides which may have been sprayed with chemicals.

Preparation and Cooking
Remove stems from nettles and wash thoroughly, still wearing rubber gloves. Shake off excess moisture and cook in a tightly-covered pan, with only the moisture clinging to the leaves after washing, for 10-15 minutes, until tender. Drain well, then chop or purée and serve as required.

Serving Suggestions
Toss in melted butter and seasonings and serve as an accompaniment, or as a base for poached eggs (Florentine-style). Good too, served with a béchamel sauce; or par-cooked and sautéed in butter with spring onions and garlic, with a little cream stirred in just before serving. Nettles also make a delicious soup (see page 75).

Rocket

Rocket (*Eruca sativa*) is native to the Mediterranean region and grows wild in many parts of Europe. Related to the cresses, rocket has pinnately-lobed leaves with a slightly hot, peppery flavour. The cultivated varieties are more tender and milder than the wild type.

Rocket may be found in Greek and Italian foodshops, and sometimes in supermarkets. It grows easily from seed and is worth planting in your garden to 'experiment' and enjoy its unusual flavour.

Snipped (sparingly) into salads, rocket is especially good, or try it combined with spring onions and tomatoes in a tangy dressing as an unusual first course. Sprinkle over soups as a flavourful garnish.

Rocket

Nettle

Dandelion

Potato

Maris bard

Maris piper

The potato (*Solanum tuberosum*) must be the most popular vegetable worldwide – yet it came to Europe as recently as the 16th century.

There are two potato crops: early or 'new' potatoes and maincrop or 'old' potatoes. Selecting the right type for a recipe is important: the 'new' or waxy types are good for salads, sautéeing and boiling, and the floury 'old' types are better for jacket baking, roasting and puréeing. There are many varieties to choose from.

Buying and Storing

New potatoes arrive in the shops in northern Europe in late spring and remain available until the end of the summer, although imported new potatoes are available at other times during the year. Test for freshness by making sure the skins rub off easily. Buy in quantities you need and use within 48 hours.

Maincrop potatoes are around from late summer to late spring. In autumn their flesh is still a little waxy but becomes less so during storage. Potatoes keep well stored in a cool frost-free place, in the large brown sacks or bags in which they come from the supplier; they are considerably cheaper bought direct from source. If purchased in polythene bags, remove and store in a cool dry, dark airy place.

Preparation and Cooking

Boil (or steam) new potatoes in their skins, or very thinly scraped, in salted water for 15 minutes, or until just tender. A sprig of mint added to the water helps bring out the flavour. If you prefer not to eat new potatoes in their skins, strip them off after cooking.

Maincrop potatoes may also be cooked in their skins, or peeled very thinly. Cut into uniform sizes, cover and cook gently in boiling salted water (or steam – they are less likely to go mushy) for 20 minutes, or until tender. Drain, return to pan and shake briefly over a low heat to dry off before using.

Serving Suggestions

Crisp, golden sautéed potatoes, cooked with onion and bacon, are delicious; so too are jacket baked potatoes served with butter, or thick sour cream and chives.

Mashed with butter and cream and a pinch of nutmeg, potatoes make a good accompaniment for rich dishes; or serve them mashed and piped in nests, Duchesse-style. Gratin Dauphinoise (potatoes layered and baked with garlic and cream) makes an ideal dinner accompaniment, as do Pommes Dauphine – puréed potatoes blended with choux paste, then piped and deep-fried to light, golden puffs.

Romano

King Edward

Pentland

Charlotte

Belle de Fontenay

Yam

The yam (*Dioscorea alata*) is a tropical tuber often mistaken for the sweet potato. Perhaps the confusion arises because sweet potatoes are known as yams in the southern states of America. Originally yams came from Africa, but many varieties are now grown in tropical countries. They can grow to enormous sizes, weighing as much as 100 kg (50 lb), but those available in western countries usually weigh around 500 g (1 lb). The large ones are often cut into smaller pieces for sale.

Yams are available all year round from West Indian and African foodshops and specialist grocers. The bark-like skin is tough and thick and varies from light to dark brown in colour. The flesh may be white, yellow or sometimes pink. Whole yams store well for several weeks in a cool, dry, dark place; if in pieces, cover with plastic wrap and use within a week.

Preparation and Cooking
Cut off thick woody skin and, if not cooking immediately, drop into a bowl of cold water with lemon juice added to prevent discoloration. Dice, slice or cut into pieces, then cook in boiling salted water for 20-30 minutes, until tender. Drain, return to pan and shake over a low heat for a few minutes to dry off.

Serving Suggestions
Serve tossed in butter flavoured with cinnamon, nutmeg and brown sugar, or purée with butter, seasonings and herbs.

Yams may also be baked in their skins and served like jacket baked potatoes; par-cooked, sliced and sautéed or frittered; or added to spicy soups, casseroles and curries.

Cassava

Cassava (*Manihot esculenta*), also known as yuca and sweet manioc, is native to the West Indies, Africa and South America. It is a strange looking starchy tuber which is long, hairy and cylindrical, tapering at one end. It is from this vegetable that we get tapioca.

Cassava is not widely available – look out for it in Asian stores. It keeps well in a cool, airy place for several weeks.

Preparation and Cooking
Peel off the hairy, bark-like skin, cut into even pieces and cook, covered, in boiling salted water for 20 minutes, or until tender.

Serving Suggestions
Serve and eat cassava as you would potatoes. As the flavour is rather bland, pep it up with herbs and seasonings – perhaps a dash of lemon juice or a little lime pickle.

Cassava is good mashed, or par-cooked then sautéed. The flesh may also be cut into chips, coated in batter, deep-fried and served with a tasty dip.

Sweet Potato

The sweet potato (*Ipomoea batatas*) was common in Europe during the 16th and 17th centuries and, in fact, came before the ordinary potato. It then gradually faded as the ordinary potato became favourite. The two are not related.

You will find sweet potatoes in supermarkets, specialist greengrocers and West Indian foodshops during winter and spring. The skin colour varies according to variety; the smooth, red-skinned type is the one usually available in Britain. Buy smooth, firm tubers and store in a cool, dry, airy place (not the refrigerator) for up to 3 days.

Preparation and Cooking
Scrub, peel and slice or cut into even pieces and simmer gently in salted water for 15-20 minutes,

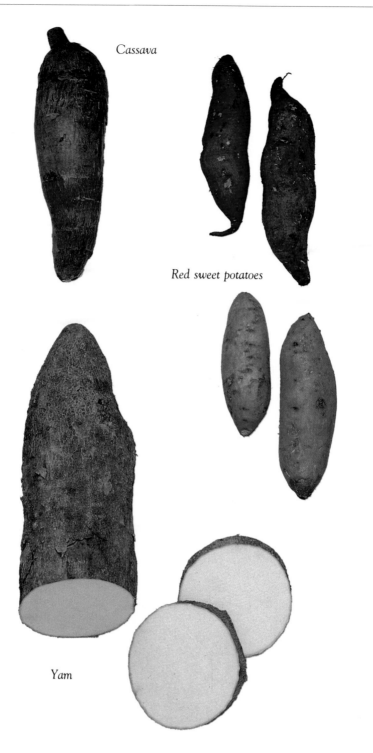

Cassava

Red sweet potatoes

Yam

until tender; the flesh is soft and floury when cooked; it will break up if boiled rapidly. Sweet potatoes may also be boiled in their skins and peeled after cooking.

Serving Suggestions
Serve sweet potatoes as you would ordinary potatoes; either boiled, mashed with butter and seasonings, or chipped and deep-fried. Their delicious sweet flavour makes them a natural for serving glazed or candied, or baked in a mixture of brown sugar, spices, butter and orange juice: cooked this way they make a perfect accompaniment for turkey or chicken. Try them baked in their jackets or roasted round the joint, too. Thin slivers of sweet potato, dipped in batter and fried, are also good (see page 89).

Jerusalem Artichoke

The Jerusalem artichoke (*Helianthus tuberosus*) is a native of North Africa and has no historical connection with Jerusalem. The word is believed to be a misinterpretation of *girasole*, the Italian name for sunflower, to which the Jerusalem artichoke is related.

There are two types, red and white; the white (actually light brown in colour) has a finer flavour and is more widely available. In season throughout the winter, Jerusalem artichokes look rather like knobbly new potatoes. Buy those that feel firm, as they soften and wrinkle with age. They will keep successfully for up to 3 days in a cool, dry, dark place.

Preparation and Cooking
Peeling Jerusalem artichokes is a fiddly job, so cook the scrubbed tubers in their skins and peel them afterwards – it's quicker and far easier.

Cook whole artichokes in lightly salted boiling water for about 10 minutes if unpeeled, 6-7 minutes if peeled; cook sliced or diced ones for 5 minutes. Artichokes may also be steamed, or cooked in their jackets in a hot oven for 30-40 minutes. Pierce with a skewer to test – they should be just tender when ready.

Serving Suggestions
Boiled or steamed artichokes are delicious left whole, tossed in lemon and parsley butter and sprinkled with crisp, crumbled bacon. Delicious too, coated with a rich cheese or tomato sauce. Puréed they make excellent soup – enriched with butter and a little cream or an egg yolk. They are very good sliced and sautéed in garlic butter or cooked Dauphinoise style (see page 104). Artichokes may also be served raw in salads: peel and grate them straight into a lemon or vinegar dressing (to prevent discoloration) before combining with other salad ingredients.

Chinese Artichoke

The Chinese artichoke (*Stachys affinis*), a native of the Far East, is especially prized in France. Chinese artichokes are smaller than Jerusalem artichokes, creamy-coloured, with tapering ends. They have a delicate flavour and are at their best served simply.

Preparation and Cooking
Wash and cook in their skins (they do not need peeling) in boiling salted water, or a little chicken stock, for 10-12 minutes, until tender but still crisp. Drain and toss in melted butter. Also good served warm with a delicate vinaigrette.

Jicama

Jicama (*Pachyrrhizus erosus*) is native to Mexico and looks rather like a turnip with a thin brown skin. It is sometimes called yam bean. Jicama varies in size from 500 g – 3 kg (1-6 lb) and is often sold cut into smaller pieces. The white flesh resembles that of the waterchestnut in taste and texture.

Buying and Storing
This vegetable is not widely available, so look out for it in specialist food shops. Choose small to medium jicama, as these have a better texture than the larger ones which can be 'woody'. The whole vegetable keeps well in a cool, dry, dark place for up to 2 weeks; cover cut pieces with plastic wrap and refrigerate for up to 1 week.

Preparation and Cooking
Scrub well in cold water, peel, then slice thinly, shred, dice or cut into julienne strips. Cook in boiling salted water for about 20 minutes, or steam, until tender. Delicious served raw in salads or as an appetizer with dips – try it stir-fried, too.

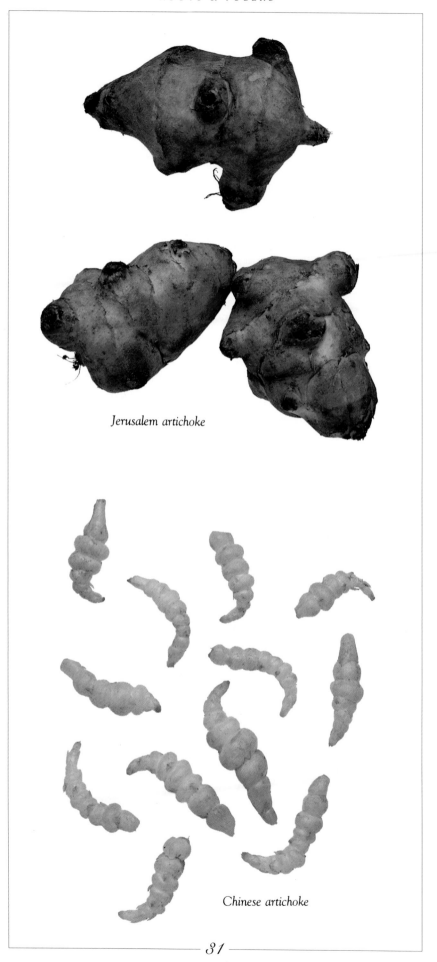

Jerusalem artichoke

Chinese artichoke

Salsify

Salsify (*Tragopogon porrifolius*) belongs to the daisy family and is a native of southern Europe. It is a long, white-fleshed root with a tender pale skin – sometimes referred to as the oyster plant because its flavour is similar to that of oysters. The flavour is wonderfully delicate and well worth trying.

Buying and Storing
Salsify is in the shops from autumn through to late spring. Look for young ones with fresh greyish-green leaves and neat tapering roots – avoid those that are limp with dry, shrivelled skins. Salsify will keep for 2 to 3 days, stored in the salad drawer of the refrigerator.

Preparation and Cooking
The leaves of salsify are edible and very good shredded raw into salads; they may also be cooked in the same way as spinach (see page 20). Scrub salsify in cold water, cut off top and tapering root end and scrape off skin. Cut into even pieces. If not cooking immediately, place in cold water with a spoonful of lemon juice or vinegar added to keep the flesh white. Cook in boiling salted water for 20-25 minutes or until tender.

Serving Suggestions
Salsify is delicious served with béarnaise or mornay sauce, or tossed in melted butter flavoured with anchovy essence. Cream of salsify soup is excellent: cook the vegetable with onions and stock until very tender, then purée and reheat with cream, seasonings and chopped herbs. Salsify fritters are extremely tasty: par-cook the vegetable in fingers or slices, then dip in a light batter, deep-fry until golden and serve with tartare or spiced tomato sauce.

To make a salad, cut salsify into small pieces and cook as above, drain and toss while still warm in a vinaigrette. Chill before mixing with sliced spring onions, herbs and corn salad.

Scorzonera

Scorzonera (*Scorzonera hispanica*), or black salsify as it is known, simply looks like a black-skinned version of salsify. Although the dark skin may look unappetizing, the flesh inside is white and tastes very similar to salsify – in fact, many people claim it has a better, more pronounced flavour.

Scorzonera is available during the winter until late spring. Prepare and cook as salsify (see above).

Eddoe

The eddoe (*Colocasia esculenta* var. *antiquorum*) is a starchy vegetable, used as a staple food in the West Indies, India and West Africa. It is called dasheen or taro in Indian and West Indian food shops, kolocassi in Greek stores.

Available in summer, eddoes come in many sizes and have a rough brown exterior. Select those which feel firm; they will keep in the salad drawer of the refrigerator for 4-5 days.

The leaves of the eddoe plant are called taro or dasheen leaves. They are large, thick and fleshy and are also available during the summer.

Preparation and Cooking
Wash, peel and slice eddoes, or cut into even pieces, and cook and serve as you would potatoes (see page 26). They may be boiled and mashed, sliced and fried, or added to casseroles and curries. Try them boiled and tossed in garlic butter with plenty of seasoning, or spiced up with a few drops of Tabasco sauce.

Taro leaves have a slightly bitter flavour and are prepared in the same way as kale (see page 14).

Eddoe (taro)

Scorzonera

Radish

The radish (*Raphanus sativus*) is an ancient vegetable believed to have originated in southern Asia, although some experts say its place of origin was Egypt.

There are many different types of radish, all varying in flavour, shape and colour. Some are hot and pungent; some are small, round and scarlet; others are elongated and paler in colour, often with white tips.

Radishes are usually quite small, although the white radish can be 15-18 cm (6-7 in) long. During the winter, Spanish or black radishes are sometimes available: these have a large bulbous root with white flesh and are stronger and coarser than the smaller types.

Buying and Preparation

Available more or less all year. Look for smooth, bright-looking radishes. The leaves wilt quickly so are not a good indication of quality. To check for freshness, it is best to squeeze radishes gently – they should feel firm, never spongy or soft. Wash and store in polythene bags in the salad drawer of the refrigerator for 4-5 days.

To prepare, trim off root ends and tops and drop into iced water for an hour or so before serving.

Serving Suggestions

The French enjoy radishes spread with butter, dipped in salt and eaten with crusty French bread. The smaller red radishes are a nice addition to salads – either whole, quartered or sliced; white and black radishes should be grated before adding to salads.

Radishes make pretty 'roses' for garnishing. To make a radish rose, trim away root ends and larger leaves – leave on the smallest leaf. Using a small, sharp pointed knife, cut 3 petals from root end to leaf end of radish, taking care not to cut right through. Place in iced water until opened out.

Radishes are also good served hot: try them sautéed or stir-fried; steamed or braised and served with a butter or cream sauce.

Mooli

The mooli (*Raphanus sativus* var. *longipinnatus*), also known as daikon, is a popular vegetable in some parts of Asia and has been grown for many centuries in China and Japan.

The mooli is closely related to the radish but it actually looks like a giant white carrot. It has a crisp, crunchy texture and a milder flavour than the more familiar red radish. Mooli is available throughout the year.

When buying mooli, go for clean, fresh ones which feel hard – limp moolis may well be spongy and dry inside. Trim root end and top, then peel thinly to prepare.

They keep well for up to a week stored in a cool, dry place or in a polythene bag in the salad drawer of the refrigerator.

Serving Suggestions

Slice or grate for adding raw to salads, or use grated as a sandwich filling – especially good with cream cheese and chopped nuts. Cut into neat fingers, raw mooli makes an excellent crudité. Grate or shred a little mooli into clear, broth-style soups to add 'bite' and flavour.

Try serving mooli as a hot accompaniment: slice and cook in lightly salted boiling water for 3-4 minutes, then drain and toss in butter or cream and freshly ground pepper. Thinly sliced, it can be stir-fried with other ingredients. Mooli is also good braised in butter and stock.

The Japanese use this vegetable frequently, often finely grated and added to dips and sauces, and carved into shapes as a garnish.

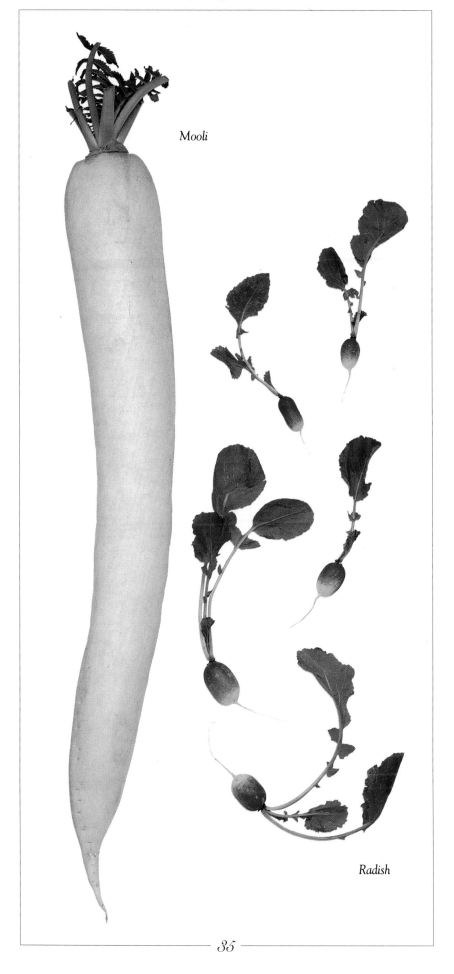

Mooli

Radish

Beetroot

Beetroot (*Beta vulgaris*) is thought to have been cultivated in the Middle East about 2000 years ago. The Greeks and Romans grew the vegetable for its leaves. Although today we enjoy beetroot for its root, the leaves are, in fact, tasty and nutritious, similar in flavour to spinach and may be cooked in the same way (see page 20).

Buying and Storing
Beetroot is available all year; the baby kind, available at their peak during summer, are especially sweet and delicious. Look for raw beetroot with smooth skins and hard roots.

Ready-cooked beetroot is also available: buy it unskinned whenever possible. Beetroot is also sold in vacuum packs, cooked and skinned and often flavoured with vinegar, so check for suitability if using them in a specific recipe.

Raw beetroot keeps well in a cool place for up to 1 week. The cooked type will keep in the refrigerator for up to 3 days.

Preparation and Cooking
Twist off leafy tops, leaving about 2.5 cm (1 in) of stems: do not trim root ends unless a recipe states otherwise. Rinse, taking care not to break the skins or beetroot will 'bleed' and lose colour during cooking. Cook in boiling salted water for 45 minutes to 1½ hours, according to size. To test if cooked, lift from pan and press gently: if skin slips off easily it is cooked. Alternatively, bake beetroot in foil in the oven as you would jacket potatoes. Peel while warm and use as required.

Serving Suggestions
Good in hot dishes and accompaniments as well as salads, relishes and pickles. Try it grated or diced and served warm in a herbed vinaigrette, or cold in a thick sour cream or yogurt dressing flavoured with horseradish or dill. Serve hot baby beetroots in a creamy béchamel or cheese sauce as an accompaniment. Beetroot is also used to make the classic Russian soup – Borsch.

Celeriac

Celeriac (*Apium graveolens*) was a popular vegetable in the 18th and 19th centuries. It became less fashionable, but is now enjoying a revival. Often called turnip-rooted celery, celeriac is native to southern Europe.

In spite of its knobbly swollen shape, celeriac is closely related to celery and has an authentic celery taste; it is similar in texture to the heart of celery. It is available during most of the winter. Select hard roots that weigh heavy in the hand. It keeps well in the salad drawer of the refrigerator for several days.

Preparation and Cooking
Peel and slice celeriac and drop into a bowl of cold water with lemon juice or vinegar added to prevent discoloration. Cook in boiling salted water for 20-30 minutes (according to size), until tender; or steam, allowing a little longer.

Serving Suggestions
Raw and coarsely grated or chopped celeriac is a delicious addition to many salads. For a starter, blanch julienne strips in acidulated water for 2 minutes; toss while still warm in a mustard-flavoured vinaigrette and serve chilled.

Cooked celeriac is marvellous for flavouring soups, stocks, casseroles and sauces, and is a splendid vegetable in its own right. Serve it hot with a hollandaise, herb or butter sauce; or par-cooked and baked *au gratin* with a rich cheese sauce.

Puréed celeriac, flavoured with nutmeg, cream and herbs, makes an excellent soup. Or mix the purée with equal quantities of mashed potato, blend with butter and seasonings, and serve sprinkled with toasted almonds. Celeriac is also delicious served French-fried style (see page 106).

Celeriac

Beetroot

Young early turnip

Maincrop purple-tinged turnip

Maincrop green-tinged turnip

Turnip

The turnip (*Brassica campestris* var. *rapa*), a prehistoric vegetable, was a staple food in northern Europe until potatoes gained in popularity. Too often this delicious vegetable is ignored or relegated to the stew-pot – it deserves more recognition.

There are two types – early and maincrop. The early type have tender flesh with a more delicate flavour than the maincrop variety and usually appear in the shops in spring through to summer; the maincrop variety follow on from summer through to spring. They may be round, flattened or cylindrical, yellow or white, often with a flash of green or purple near the top. Choose firm, young turnips that feel heavy for their size. They store well in a cool, dry place or refrigerator for 1-2 weeks.

Preparation and Cooking
Trim top and root, then peel. Cook young turnips whole, quartered or sliced, either by steaming or boiling in salted water until tender. The timing varies with the age of the vegetable, but as a general guide, steam young whole turnips for 20-30 minutes; boil older types for 20 minutes if sliced, or 30-40 minutes if whole.

Serving Suggestions
Enjoy turnips boiled, braised, added to casseroles, pot roasts and pies – and even raw. The light and delicate, slightly peppery flavour goes splendidly with butter and rich creamy sauces.

For a colourful combination, try thin julienne strips of carrot and turnip poached in stock and served tossed in double (thick) cream and chives. Puréed turnip mixed with mashed potato, butter and seasoning makes a lovely topping for fish pies and an unusual accompaniment for smoked sausages or meat and poultry dishes.

Whole baby turnips, par-cooked, hollowed out and filled with a tasty mixture before baking, are quite delicious (see page 91).

Coarsely grate or sliver young raw turnips and add to salads. They are especially good with watercress and orange, or try them dressed with a tangy vinaigrette or mixed into a mayonnaise potato salad.

Swede

Swede (*Brassica campestris* var. *ruta-baga*) or Swedish turnip is sometimes confused with turnip, although it is larger and sweeter with orangy-yellow flesh. Swedes are believed to have originated in Bohemia in the 17th century.

These purple-orange skinned roots are in season during winter and spring. Choose medium swedes – large ones can sometimes be woody or pithy. They store well in a cool, dry place for several weeks.

Preparation and Cooking
Cut into quarters for easy handling, then peel and slice or dice evenly. Cooking time varies according to age but, as a guide, cook in boiling salted water for 15-20 minutes or until tender; steaming takes a little longer. Drain well, return to pan and shake over a low heat to evaporate any liquid remaining.

Serving Suggestions
Bashed neeps – the traditional accompaniment to haggis – is probably one of the most famous ways of serving swede. This dish of cooked, well-mashed swede, seasoned with salt, nutmeg and plenty of black pepper, with a generous knob of butter or a spoonful of cream added before serving, is delicious. Slivers of raw swede are an essential item in a traditional Cornish pasty.

Try swede sliced and par-boiled then finished in a butter and honey glaze, or diced and braised in butter and stock, flavoured with chopped parsley. Thin julienne strips, par-cooked and added to stir-fry dishes, make a pleasant change.

Swede

Carrot

The carrot (*Daucus carota*) originated in Afghanistan and first arrived in England from Holland. Carrots are in season all year, with baby new carrots – young or early carrots – around in early summer. These are usually sold in bunches with the foliage attached. Choose firm bunches with fresh greenery. Maincrop carrots are larger and sold trimmed. Carrots store well in a cool place for several days, but remove plastic bags or they 'sweat'.

Preparation and Cooking

There is no need to peel baby carrots – simply scrub, top and tail, then cook whole in boiling salted water or steam, for 10-15 minutes, until tender. Cooked this way they are delicious served tossed in butter with a sprinkling of fresh herbs.

Maincrop carrots have a stronger, richer flavour. Peel only very thinly, then quarter, slice or cut into julienne strips and boil or steam until tender. Carrots are also delicious par-cooked and finished by sautéeing and glazing in butter.

Serving Suggestions

Carrots can be served in a variety of ways: as accompaniments; puréed in soups and soufflés; braised; added to casseroles and pot roasts; or served raw.

Baby carrots are delicious raw for dunking into dips, or grated into a tangy dressing as a starter or side salad. For a refreshingly simple salad, cut carrots into thin strips, mix with orange-flavoured mayonnaise or walnut oil dressing and arrange on a bed of mixed salad leaves. A little raw grated carrot forked into boiled rice just before serving adds interest and texture.

Raw maincrop carrots add texture and flavour to various cakes and puddings – many Christmas pudding recipes include a little raw grated carrot to help keep the pud moist during storage.

As interesting accompaniments, serve carrots hot in a cream sauce flavoured with cinnamon; mashed with puréed parsnips, enriched with butter and cream; glazed in sugar or honey; or stir-fried.

Parsnip

The parsnip (*Pastinaca sativa*) is thought to be native to the Eastern Mediterranean. Its distinctive sweet flavour is an acquired taste – it seems to be the vegetable you either love or loathe.

Parsnips are available from autumn until late spring – their flavour is said to be improved if they have been touched by frost. Choose small to medium sizes rather than large ones which may have woody centre cores. They should have a crisp, clean look. Parsnips keep for up to 5 days in the refrigerator, or for 3-4 days in a cool dry place.

Preparation and Cooking

Scrub and trim tops and root ends, then peel or scrape thinly. Small ones may be left whole; otherwise halve, quarter or slice, discarding cores from larger parsnips. Cook in boiling salted water, or steam, for 15-25 minutes, depending on size, until tender. Drain well, return to pan and place over a low heat for a few minutes to dry off.

Serving Suggestions

One of the nicest and most popular ways to cook parsnips is to par-boil them, then roast around the joint. Young parsnips are good steamed and served with a creamy herbed sauce, or par-boiled, dipped in batter and fried – or even chipped, deep-fried and sprinkled with parsley.

Parsnips, mashed to a smooth purée with butter, cream and a little sherry and sprinkled with toasted pine nuts, create a splendid dinner party accompaniment. Another delicious idea is to cut parsnips into thin strips, wrap in a well-buttered foil parcel with plenty of seasoning and cook in a moderate oven for 45 minutes, or until tender.

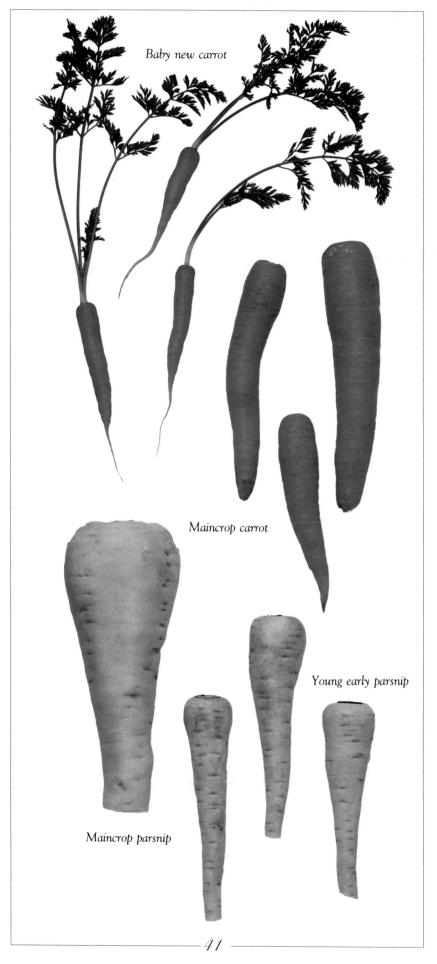

Baby new carrot

Maincrop carrot

Young early parsnip

Maincrop parsnip

Onion

The onion (*Allium cepa*) has been around for at least 5,000 years and is thought to have originated in Central Asia. The genus *Allium* includes onions of all sizes: maincrop, Spanish, Breton, Italian red, pickling onions, spring onions, shallots and also garlic.

Maincrop onions: These are the most commonly available and are in the shops all year. They are strongly-flavoured and come in a range of sizes, according to type. The pungent white flesh is encased in layers of papery brown or beige/white skin.

Spanish and Breton onions: These are large and round (larger than the maincrop onion) and have a milder, sweeter flavour – delicious eaten raw. Available all year.

Italian red onions: These are easily recognized by their red skins and red-tinged flesh, which is mild and sweet. They vary in size. Red onions are not as widely available as other types; look out for them in specialist greengrocers and Greek and Italian foodshops.

Pickling onions: Also called button onions, these are small maincrop onions which are picked while the bulbs are immature. They have a strong, pungent flavour. Although generally used for pickling, they enhance many cooked dishes and may be substituted for shallots in recipes, although the flavour will be less delicate. Pickling onions are in the shops during autumn and early winter.

Spring onions: These are onion sets of seed onions, harvested when young and green before the bulb has had time to form properly. Tender and mild with small white bulbs and green leaves, they are essentially a salad vegetable. They are often called green shallots or simply shallots in Australia.

Shallots: These grow in tightly-packed clusters of small bulbs. They are similar in size to pickling onions but slightly elongated in shape with a finer, more delicate flavour. They are much favoured by the French in their cooking. Shallots are usually available in summer. In Australia these onions are brown shallots; the term 'shallot' is often used to describe spring onion.

Buying and Storing
Choose firm onions, with dry skins and store in a cool, dry place. Maincrop, Spanish, Breton, Italian red, pickling onions and shallots will keep for several weeks or even months if strung and hung up. Choose spring onions with a crisp, fresh appearance and store in a cool place for 2-3 days.

Preparation and Cooking
Trim root end and top from onions and remove skin, then slice or chop as required. Blanch onions in boiling water for 2-3 minutes at this stage to reduce their pungency, if wished; blanching also makes them less indigestible. Drain well and pat dry before using.

Top and tail pickling onions and, if wished, cover with boiling water for 5 minutes; drain and remove skins, which will slip off.

Simply trim root end and neaten leafy tops of spring onions and remove any damaged outer layers.

Top and tail shallots, then peel before using as required.

Onions are a versatile vegetable and are delicious roasted, glazed, boiled, sautéed, stir-fried, pickled or made into chutneys.

Serving Suggestions
Use the mild, sweet-flavoured onions raw in salads, or enjoy them sliced and served on crusty buttered bread, sprinkled with coarse salt.

Try shallots glazed in butter, white wine and herbs; add pickling onions whole to dishes such as Coq au Vin, or serve them sautéed in butter, or braised with tomatoes as a tasty accompaniment to pork and beef dishes.

Mild Spanish or Breton onions, thinly sliced and cooked in a

Breton onion

Maincrop onion

Shallot

Italian red onion

Pickling onion

Spring onion

creamy Madeira sauce, make an excellent vegetable course. French Onion Soup is always popular; for a change, make a smooth cream soup or a thick chowder.

French Onion Tart and Pissaladière – two classic onion dishes – make the perfect hors d'oeuvre, lunch or supper dish. As well as being good in salads, as crudités, or as a pretty garnish, mild and tender spring onions are also excellent thinly sliced and added to all manner of stir-fry dishes.

To make spring onion flowers: trim onions and 'feather' the leafy ends, then drop into a bowl of iced water and leave to curl and open out. These are a popular garnish for Chinese dishes.

Purple-skinned garlic

White-skinned garlic

Garlic

Garlic (*Allium sativum*), a close relative of the onion, is believed to be native to Central Asia and is one of the oldest of the edible *alliums*. Today garlic is grown throughout the world, with supplies to Britain coming from France, Italy and Spain.

Garlic cloves (or bulbs) grow in clusters known as heads. Garlic is available all year and, according to type, the cloves may be white or purple-skinned.

Buying and Storing
Select heads of garlic which feel fat and firm, checking to see that the cloves have not dried out. Garlic stores well in a dry, airy place for several weeks.

Preparation and Cooking
Break off the required number of cloves, skin, then slice, chop or crush as required. To crush, place cloves on a board, sprinkle with salt and, using the flat side of a knife, mash to form a smooth paste; or use a garlic press.

Although garlic may be served as a vegetable, it is more often used as a flavouring. Garlic may be used either raw or cooked: when raw it has a strong, intense flavour; once cooked, the flavour becomes less pungent; after long, slow cooking, garlic becomes surprisingly mellow and sweet.

Serving Suggestions
Peel the cloves from one or two heads of garlic and cook them around a chicken or lamb joint when pot-roasting – the result will be deliciously sweet and succulent. Use one or two heads of peeled garlic cloves to great effect in garlic soups, and rich fish soups and stews – to impart a marvellous sweetness and flavour. Whole peeled cloves of garlic, simmered gently in milk until tender, then strained, make an extremely good accompaniment to grilled steaks and chops.

The list of ideas for using garlic as a flavouring is almost endless: rub a cut clove around a salad bowl before filling to give a delicate flavour, or steep a cut garlic clove in the salad dressing for an hour or so before serving.

Rub steaks, chops and chicken portions with a cut garlic clove (or a little crushed garlic for a stronger flavour) before grilling, barbecueing or frying. Nick the skin of lamb joints and insert thin slivers of garlic before roasting. Add a crushed clove of garlic to casseroles, soups and stews to enhance the flavour of other ingredients.

Use garlic to flavour dips, pâtés, marinades and sauces, such as pesto to serve with pasta; or dressings, such as aïoli; or butter to make garlic bread and include chopped herbs for a change.

Leek

The leek (*Allium porrum*) has been around for thousands of years and was reputed to be one of the earliest cultivated vegetables. Leeks were popular in Egypt at the time of the Pharoahs, and with the Romans.

Main supplies are available from autumn through to early spring, though they are considered to be at their best during the winter.

Buying and Storing
Choose straight leeks with equal proportions of green top and white stalk. Small and medium leeks are more tender than large ones. Store, unwrapped, in a cool, dark, airy place for up to 3 days.

Preparation and Cooking
Trim off root end and a little of the green top and remove tough outer leaves. Wash thoroughly: if in any doubt as to whether they are completely clean, slit the leek down one side and hold, root end upwards, under cold running water, letting the water run through the layers. Drain upside down. Leave whole, halve, slice or finely shred.

The best ways of cooking this delicious vegetable are braising in butter with a little stock or water, or steaming. Take care not to overcook, as they easily become mushy and lose shape. Braise or simmer whole young leeks for 8-10 minutes; steam for 15 minutes; allow a little longer for thicker ones.

Serving Suggestions
Leeks are excellent served hot or cold, raw or cooked. When young and tender, try them raw in salads – either shredded finely or very thinly sliced and separated into rings. Or steam, then chill and serve in a herbed vinaigrette. Cooked *à la grecque*, they are delicious served hot or chilled. Or par-cook, coat with a cheese sauce and bake until golden. Chopped leeks in a cheese sauce make a good filling for pancakes or filo parcels. Try sliced leeks baked with eggs, cream and ham in a quiche or pie. Leeks are particularly good in soups, notably the classic Vichyssoise.

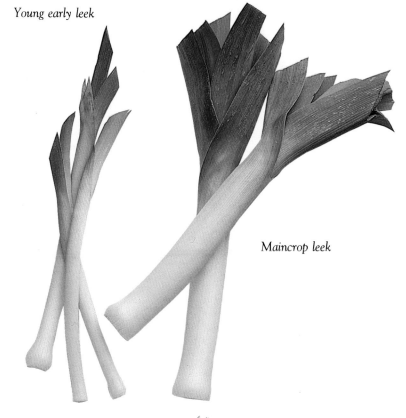

Young early leek

Maincrop leek

Green Pea

The pea (*Pisum sativum* var. *hortense*) was one of the earliest vegetables grown by man and for centuries 'field peas' were dried to provide a staple food during winter months. Not until the 16th century did garden peas (developed in Italy) reach northern Europe.

There are two basic types of shelling pea: the ordinary garden pea and the larger marrowfat pea, more generally used for canning and drying. Green-podded garden peas are picked when 7.5-10 cm (3-4 in) long. The smallest, sweetest, and by far the most aristocratic of the shelling peas, is the *petit pois* which is picked when very young and tender. Peas are available fresh from spring through to late summer.

Buying and Storing
Choose firm, bright, crisp green pods which are well-filled; avoid any large ones with peas showing through. Best eaten fresh, although they can be stored in their pods in the salad drawer of the refrigerator for 2 days.

Preparation and Cooking
Remove peas from pods and cook in boiling salted water for 5-10 minutes, according to size, until tender but still with a 'bite'. Or steam for 10-15 minutes. Add a sprig of mint to bring out the flavour, if desired. Drain and, if using cold, plunge into cold water, then drain again – this retains the bright colour.

Serving Suggestions
When very young and sweet, raw peas can be added to salads.

Cooked peas, tossed in butter or cream and sprinkled with mint, make a simple but excellent accompaniment. Or try *Petits Pois à la Française* – braised, buttered peas, with shallots and shredded lettuce.

Serve a purée of cooked peas, flavoured with cream or bacon fat and topped with fried croûtons, as an accompaniment, or use to fill pasties, pancakes or omelettes.

Fresh pea soup is quite delicious, served hot or cold. Try cold, cooked peas in mayonnaise, served in hollowed-out tomatoes; or use cooked peas in quiches and tartlets.

Mange Tout (Snow Pea)

Mange tout (snow pea) (*Pisum sativum* var. *sacharatum*) is an edible-podded pea cultivated for its tender, succulent pod. The name mange tout means 'eat-all' in French. They have a flat pod about 7.5-10 cm (3-4 in) long and about 2.5 cm (1 in) wide. The peas inside are very tiny.

Mange tout (snow peas) are now available more or less throughout the year, but are often rather expensive. The pods should look fresh green and feel crisp. They are at their best eaten fresh, but will keep in a polythene bag in the refrigerator for 24 hours.

Preparation and Cooking
These peas are delicate so should be handled with care. Simply top and tail very young pods; more mature pods require stringing. Leave whole or slice, according to recipe.

Stir-frying is probably the best way to cook them, or they can be steamed for 5-10 minutes with a knob of butter, until just tender. Mange tout (snow peas) may also be cooked in boiling salted water for just 2 minutes; drain thoroughly before serving.

Serving Suggestions
Very young and tender mange tout (snow peas) can be served raw, whole or sliced, in salads. They are popular in Chinese stir-fried dishes. For a simple accompaniment, add them to hot oil, flavoured with garlic or fresh root (green) ginger, and stir-fry for 2-3 minutes.

Steamed or boiled mange tout (snow peas) are delicious served with a hollandaise sauce or tossed in melted butter or sesame oil. They are also very tasty served cold in a vinaigrette.

Mange tout (snow pea)

Sugar snap pea

Sugar Snap Pea

The sugar snap pea (*Pisum sativum* var. *axiphium*) is a relatively new variety of edible-podded pea. It has a thicker pod than the mange tout (snow pea) with well developed seeds. The sugar snap pea has a sweet flavour. Select, prepare and cook as for mange tout (snow peas).

Asparagus Pea

The asparagus pea (*Lotus tetragonolobus*), or 'winged pea', is not a true pea but, like the mange tout (snow pea) is eaten pod and all. It has a mild, delicate asparagus flavour. The pods should be picked when very young. Prepare and cook as for mange tout (snow pea).

Broad Bean

The broad bean (*Vicia faba*) is one of the oldest of cultivated vegetables and is thought to have come from the East, although its exact origin is obscure. Broad beans have been eaten in Britain for centuries; fortunately the modern varieties are a great improvement on the tough bean of times past. They are known as Fava beans in Italy and America.

They grow in large thick pods with a soft, furry lining and are available from mid-spring through to late summer. Buy soft, tender, bright green pods that are not too large and puffy. Best used fresh, although they may be stored in a polythene bag in the salad drawer of the refrigerator for up to 2 days.

Preparation and Cooking
Unless very young and tender, broad beans need shelling from pods. Once the beans are larger than a big pea, their skins are coarse and tough and should also be removed. Skin beans raw or after cooking, when cool enough to handle: slit the skin along the indented edge of the bean, then squeeze to remove the bean.

To cook, simmer in just enough lightly salted water to cover, with a knob of butter added, for 8-10 minutes or until tender.

Serving Suggestions
When very young and no more than 7.5 cm (3 in) long, broad beans in their pods are tender enough to eat raw. They are delicious as 'dipping' sticks, served with aïoli, or served in salad.

Toss and heat cooked, drained broad beans in garlic butter or cream and fresh herbs, or serve with a parsley or cheese sauce.

A purée of broad beans, mixed with butter and cream, makes a delicious accompaniment (good with boiled gammon), or it may be turned into a rich soup with a cheese topping (see page 77).

For a salad, drain cooked broad beans and toss while still hot in a well-seasoned vinaigrette; chill before serving. If preferred, cool, then mix into a lemon mayonnaise or serve in a potato salad, flavoured with finely grated lemon rind.

Runner Bean

The runner bean (*Phaseolus coccineus*), native to South America, was brought to Britain in the early 17th century. For many years, runner beans were grown in Britain for their beauty as an ornamental plant, not as a vegetable!

Runner beans have large, flat bright green succulent pods which need stringing before cooking. They are more popular in Britain than the French bean and are widely grown by keen gardeners.

Available from mid-summer until the beginning of autumn, fresh runner beans should snap in two when bent. They will keep well in a polythene bag in the salad drawer of the refrigerator for 2-3 days.

Preparation and Cooking
Top, tail and string young beans; more mature beans are best thinly pared all the way round to avoid any stringiness. Cut into thin slices or short diagonal lengths. Cook in boiling salted water for 5-12 minutes, until tender, according to size and age. Or steam, allowing a few minutes extra cooking. Drain well and return to pan over a low heat for a few seconds to dry off.

Serving Suggestions
The simplest way to enjoy these beans is to add salt and pepper to taste and a good knob of butter, or a spoonful or two of cream, and heat through gently, tossing until beans are evenly coated. Runner beans are also good cooked *à la grecque*, or blanched and stir-fried.

They are delicious in salads, relishes and pickles, and can be added with other vegetables to hot soups or rice or pasta mixtures. They may also be served as French beans (see page 50).

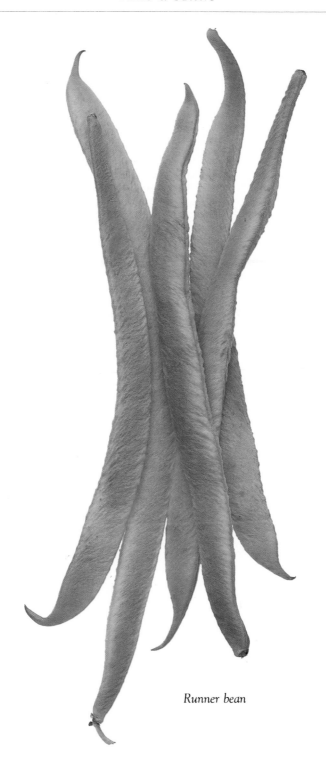

Runner bean

Lima Bean

The lima bean (*Phaseolus lunatus*), also known as Madagascar bean, is native to Lima, Peru. Lima beans are normally found fresh only in the tropical areas where they grow.

These beans are flat and kidney-shaped. They are shelled and cooked as broad beans (opposite). Although not widely available in Britain, they are available frozen from specialist shops; lima beans are also available dried and canned.

French Bean

The French bean (*Phaseolus vulgaris*), also known as the kidney bean, haricot vert, green bean and stringless bean, originated in Central and South America. It arrived in Europe early in the 16th century. There are numerous varieties; most of the common ones have slender green pods, tapering to a small tail. The Dwarf bean and Bobbi bean varieties are thicker though similar in shape. Most of these beans are stringless when young.

French beans are more or less available all year, but can be expensive in winter. Buy beans of the same size and thickness to ensure even cooking; they should be fresh enough to snap in half. If not using immediately, store in salad drawer of refrigerator for 2-3 days.

Preparation and Cooking
Top and tail, and string beans if necessary. Drop into boiling salted water, cover and cook for about 5 minutes or until tender-crisp, depending on size. Or steam for 10-12 minutes, if preferred. Drain, return to pan over a low heat for a few minutes to dry off. If serving cold, drain and plunge beans into cold water, then drain again – this helps preserve a good colour.

Serving Suggestions
Cold, cooked beans are excellent dressed with a herbed vinaigrette and served as a first course, or added to salads, such as Salade Niçoise – a traditional favourite.

Sauté hot beans with small slivers of bacon and crushed garlic until bacon is crisp and golden. Toss hot beans in melted butter and seasonings, then sprinkle liberally with grated Parmesan cheese and crisp buttery crumbs. Delicious too, sautéed with button mushrooms and topped with toasted almonds. Try them in a garlicky tomato sauce, sprinkled with mozzarella cheese and flashed under the grill. Or sauté in olive oil with slivers of skinned tomato and red pepper and serve with grilled steaks.

Beansprout

The mung bean (*Phaseolus mungo*) is the bean most commonly used for producing beansprouts, although a number of other beans are also used for the same purpose. The mung bean is native to India, where the beans (not the shoots) are cooked and puréed to provide a staple food.

Beansprouts are the young, tender shoots of the bean and are very crisp and nutritious. They can be grown all year round – and are fun and simple to grow at home.

At one time, beansprouts were rather hard to find – Chinese supermarkets were about the only places selling them. Now, however, they are widely available from supermarkets and greengrocers, sold loose or in packets. They are at their best when fresh, but may be kept for 24 hours in the refrigerator.

Preparation and Cooking
Homegrown beansprouts only need washing before using, but it is now recommended that shop-bought beansprouts are blanched before use: cover with boiling water and leave for 30-45 seconds. (They will still be crisp.) Drain well, then use as required.

Serving Suggestions
Raw beansprouts add crunchiness and an interesting flavour to salads and make a welcome change in sandwich fillings.

Stir-frying is a good way of cooking beansprouts, as they must be cooked quickly to enjoy their crispness and delicate flavour. Try them stir-fried on their own or flavoured with a little ginger and sprinkled with soy sauce and sesame oil, or combine with other ingredients.

Add beansprouts to clear soups a minute or two before serving. Or make into fritters: fold beansprouts into a thick, garlicky batter and deep-fry briefly until golden; serve hot with soy or chilli sauce.

Bobbi bean

Dwarf bean

Haricot vert

Beansprout

Asparagus

Asparagus (*Asparagus officinalis*) is a member of the lily family, the edible parts being the immature shoots of the tuberous root. It is thought to have originated in the eastern Mediterranean and Asia Minor and was a favourite with the ancient Greeks and Romans.

The home-grown asparagus season is very short in the northern hemisphere – mid-spring to early summer. Imported asparagus is in the shops throughout the year.

Asparagus is a choice but expensive vegetable, sold loose or in bundles, usually graded according to thickness of stems. It can be thick or thin, light or dark green, and sometimes green and purple. The top grade has fat, tender stalks; the thinner variety (sometimes sold as sprue) is less expensive and still very good to eat.

Buying and Storing
When selecting asparagus, look for crisp stalks and tight, plump, well formed buds – avoid woody and dry stems. Asparagus is best eaten soon after purchase as it is very perishable. It will keep in the salad drawer of the refrigerator for up to 2 days (do not wash first).

Preparation and Cooking
Fresh young asparagus is tender for most of its length. Bend each stem until it snaps – the break will come at the point where the stem begins to toughen. Young green spears need only barely trimming at the cut end to neaten. Thicker spears need trimming where the stalk begins to feel tough: using a vegetable peeler, shave off the woody parts at the cut end, then trim to make all the same length. Rinse stalks in cold water and tie in bundles of about 12 with tips level.

The stalks take longer to cook than the tips and to cook successfully they should stand upright in enough simmering salted water to reach two-thirds up the stems – so the tougher stalks boil while the tender tips steam more gently. Improvize with a domed 'lid' of foil if you haven't a deep enough saucepan. An asparagus pan, specifically designed for the job, is ideal. It is tall, narrow and lined with a basket or perforated inner container which can be lifted out.

Cooking time varies according to the thickness and quality of asparagus: allow 8-12 minutes for tender young spears; 12-20 minutes for larger spears. Asparagus should be tender-crisp when ready (never floppy): test by spearing a stalk with the point of a sharp knife. Drain thoroughly, lift bundle from pan, cut string and place asparagus on a clean folded tea-towel for a few seconds to absorb moisture.

Serving Suggestions
Asparagus is delicious served hot, or warm – it's far easier to hold in the fingers for dipping into sauces – or cold. Serve it with melted butter, flavoured with lemon juice and pepper, or with a rich hollandaise or mousseline sauce.

Try asparagus coated with a Gruyère sauce and grilled until golden, or served on top of creamy scrambled eggs. Delicious too, stir-fried, puréed in a cream soup, set in dainty mousses, or used as an attractive open sandwich topping or vol-au-vent filling for buffets.

Cardoon

Cardoon (*Cynara cardunculus*), a native of the Mediterranean region, was a popular vegetable in Britain and France in the 17th and 18th centuries. It is closely related to the globe artichoke and is similar in flavour, but cardoon is cultivated more for its leafy stalks, which are blanched (just like celery) during growing.

Cardoon is in season during autumn and early winter. Look for firm, fresh, translucent stalks. Washed and trimmed, it will keep well in a polythene bag in the refrigerator for up to 5 days.

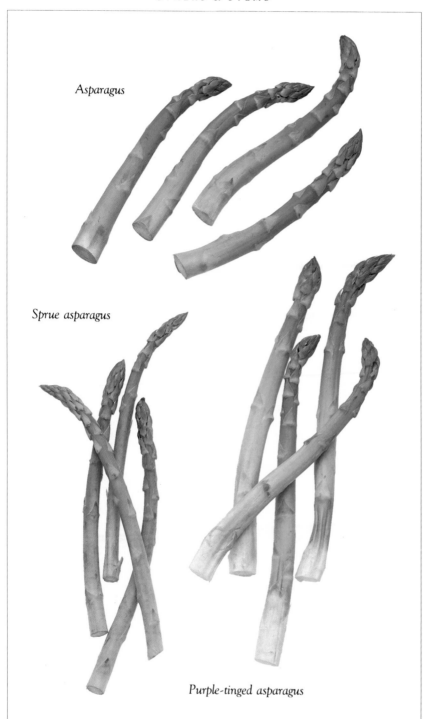

Asparagus

Sprue asparagus

Purple-tinged asparagus

Preparation and Cooking

Trim off root end, discard tough outer stems and leaves; cut prickles from inner stalks. Separate stalks and heart; cut stalks into lengths.

To eat raw, remove strings and inner white skin from stalks and slice heart thinly; rub with a cut lemon to prevent discoloration (or place in water with lemon juice added); pat dry before serving.

Cook cardoon in simmering water for 25-30 minutes, or braise in a moderate oven for 1-1¼ hours.

Serving Suggestions

Eat stalks and heart raw, like celery, with dips such as *aïoli*, or slice into salads and toss in a tangy dressing.

Enjoy cardoons hot with melted butter or a cheese or cream sauce; such as *velouté*. Also extremely good served *au gratin*, or tossed in a mixture of butter, cream and grated Parmesan. The hearts are delicious, boiled until tender, then served cold in a herbed mayonnaise or vinaigrette as a first course.

Celery

Celery (*Apium graveolens* var. *dulce*) is native to Europe. It was held in high regard, both as a food and medicinally, with the Ancient Greeks, Romans and Egyptians. However, the crisp, succulent celery we know today is the result of 16th century Italian gardeners, who developed it from the bitter-tasting weed of years ago.

Celery is available in the shops all year. There are many varieties, including the white (blanched) and light to dark green types. The green types are becoming more popular for their distinctive flavour and lack of stringiness.

Buying and Storing
Choose compact heads with firm sticks and plump bases. Leaves should be brightly coloured and fresh looking. Store unwashed celery, loosely wrapped, in the salad drawer of the refrigerator for up to 5 days. To crisp and revive wilted celery, soak in ice cold water for 1 hour before serving.

Preparation and Cooking
Trim off base and separate sticks. Scrub and rinse clean and remove leaves and any 'strings'.

To prepare celery hearts, break off outer sticks, leaving a crisp cluster of smaller, tender, tightly packed sticks about 5 cm (2 in) thick. Cut off tops to give portions measuring about 15 cm (6 in) in length. Leave whole or cut in half lengthwise and wash well. Cook in boiling salted water for about 20 minutes until tender, or steam or braise allowing a little longer.

Serving Suggestions
Tender, young celery is best eaten raw in salads or included in crudités with a selection of dips. Pieces of celery are delicious stuffed with a filling, such as cream cheese and walnuts, or taramasalata.

Celery also adds flavour and interest to casseroles, stuffings, rice and pasta dishes. Stir-frying is a quick way to cook thinly sliced celery and one which preserves its colour, flavour and texture: try sprinkling with toasted cashews and a little sesame oil before serving.

Celery hearts, blanched in boiling water for 10 minutes, then braised in stock on a bed of onions and bacon, make a good accompaniment. Or braise, then bake with a cheese or tomato sauce.

Florence Fennel

Florence fennel (*Foeniculum vulgare* var. *dulce*), also known as Florentine or sweet fennel, is a native of the Mediterranean region. It is a bulbous-shaped vegetable with a swollen, ribbed leaf base (also called a bulb or head). The texture is crisp with a flavour of aniseed. It is delicious served raw or cooked.

Florence fennel is available all year. Buy bulbs which are well-rounded in shape and pale green to white in colour – avoid any which are dark green. They will keep for up to 5 days in a polythene bag in the refrigerator.

Preparation and Cooking
If the bulb has leafy fronds at the top, save these for garnishing or adding to salads. Trim base, cut off thin ends of stalks, then halve, quarter, slice, or chop, as required.

Cook in boiling salted water for about 15 minutes until tender but still crisp. Or steam, braise or sauté in butter.

Serving Suggestions
Fennel is extremely good teamed with fish and shellfish. Try it raw or par-boiled and grated in seafood cocktails, or add to a salad and toss in a garlicky vinaigrette or mayonnaise. It is also good simmered in lightly salted water until just tender, then served drizzled with melted herb butter; tossed in cream; or sprinkled with lemon juice and black pepper. Baked Italian-style (see page 94) or cooked *à la grecque*, fennel is equally good.

White (blanched) celery

Green celery

Florence fennel

Seakale

Seakale (*Crambe maritima*) is native to Britain, where it grows wild along the coasts, and to most coastal regions of western Europe. It has been eaten for centuries.

Seakale is rarely seen in the shops, so to enjoy this sweet and succulent vegetable you will need to collect it yourself.

Preparation and Cooking
Wash thoroughly and trim off earthy stalks. The young leaves may be left on or trimmed off, if wished, and used in salads. Tie the stalks in bunches and simmer, on their sides, in salted water or chicken stock for about 25 minutes, until tender; steam if preferred. Take care not to overcook this vegetable or it will toughen. Drain well.

Serving Suggestions
The leaves of seakale are delicious shredded or chopped into salads or they may be cooked like spinach (see page 20).

Enjoy seakale stalks in the same way as you would asparagus spears: hot with a melted butter and lemon sauce, hollandaise or a creamy béchamel. For an accompaniment, arrange partially cooked stalks in a flameproof dish, coat with cheese sauce, grated cheese and crumbs and bake until golden brown.

Mushroom

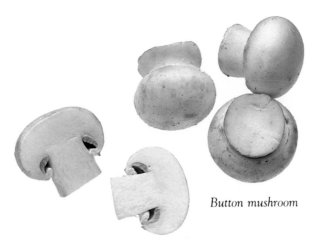

Button mushroom

Mushrooms have been around for thousands of years, but it was less than three centuries ago that man discovered how to cultivate this delicious edible fungi. The mushroom cultivated in the West *(Agaricus bisporus)* is closely related to the field mushroom *(Agaricus campestris)*. Cultivated mushrooms are available all year round.

Button mushrooms are small, white and tightly closed, with a delicate flavour.

Cup and **open cup mushrooms** are simply button types which have been left to grow larger. When still closed underneath (so that the gills cannot be seen) they are known as 'cups', but when the white skin round the stalk breaks away exposing the gills, they become 'open cups'. Both types have a fuller flavour than the button type.

Open mushrooms are more mature, the next stage in growth from 'cup' and 'open cup'.

Flat mushrooms are fully matured, with darker 'gills'. Both open and flat types have a rich flavour.

Oyster mushrooms and **Chestnut browns** are relatively new cultivated varieties.

Buying and Storing

Provided mushrooms are fresh when purchased they store well (in the punnet or paper bag in which they were bought) in the refrigerator for 2-3 days. Always remove mushrooms from polythene bags to prevent them becoming sticky.

Preparation and Cooking

There is no need to peel cultivated mushrooms, whatever their size – unless you prefer. A wipe with a clean damp cloth to remove dirt should be sufficient. For a large quantity, place in a colander and rinse very quickly under cold running water, then dry on absorbent kitchen paper. Trim stalk ends to neaten.

Mushrooms can be left whole, quartered, sliced or chopped, according to recipe. The stalks need to be removed from large flat types for grilling or stuffing. Mushrooms are naturally tender, so require little cooking.

Serving Suggestions

Mushrooms are good eaten raw in salads or served with dips as crudités. They are also delicious marinated in a lemony vinaigrette, as a first course. Large flat mushrooms, piled high with a tasty stuffing and grilled or baked, make a popular starter.

Mushrooms are delicious in quiches or cooked *à la grecque* with tomatoes, herbs and garlic. Serve sautéed mushrooms – on their own or mixed into a rich cream sauce – on toast as a tasty snack. Button mushrooms lend their delicate flavour perfectly to sauces and soups; they are especially good teamed with sherry or wine. Use the button variety too in kebabs, or try them dipped in batter and deep-fried until golden (see page 89).

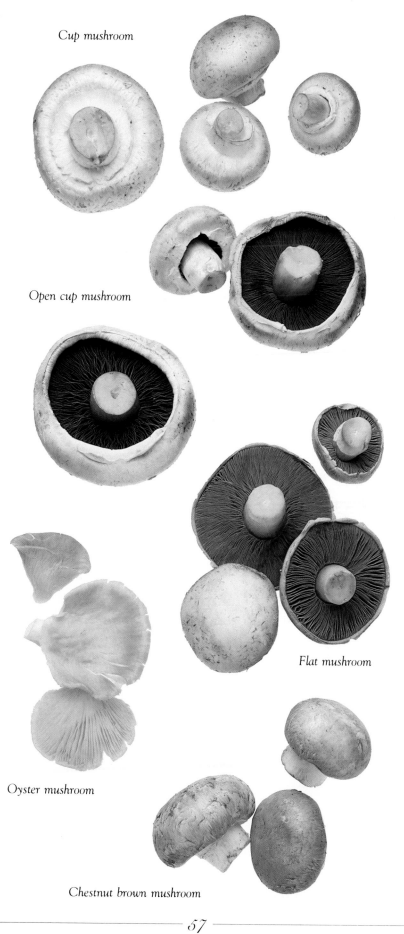

Cup mushroom

Open cup mushroom

Flat mushroom

Oyster mushroom

Chestnut brown mushroom

Tomato

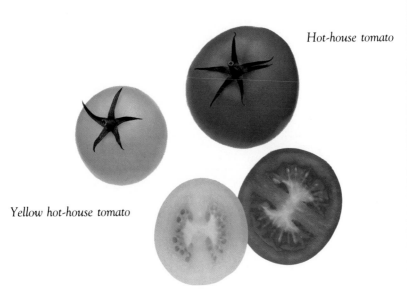

Hot-house tomato

Yellow hot-house tomato

The tomato (*Lycopersicon esculentum*) is actually a fruit, but is used as a vegetable. It originated in South America and arrived in Europe less than four centuries ago. At first, tomatoes were grown simply as decorative garden plants, as they were considered dangerous to eat being related to poisonous plants of the *Solanaceae* family, including Deadly Nightshade.

Tomatoes are available all year. Home-grown ones are available from mid-spring through summer. There are many interesting varieties to choose from.

The very smallest is the **cherry tomato** – it's tiny, sweet, crisp and juicy. **Plum (Roma) tomatoes** are fleshy and elongated; although sometimes available fresh, they are more familiar in peeled and canned form. **Beefsteak (Bullock) tomatoes** are large and 'beefy' and extremely tasty. Yellow tomato varieties are becoming more widely available.

Buying and Storing
Choose firm tomatoes – ripe if to be eaten immediately – or a little under-ripe for eating in a few days. The flavour is better if tomatoes are not refrigerated.

Preparation
Many recipes require tomatoes to be skinned and seeded. To do this, put tomatoes in a bowl and cover with boiling water. Leave to stand for 30-60 seconds, according to ripeness, then drain and peel off skins. To seed tomatoes, cut in half or quarters and scoop out seeds using a teaspoon.

To make tomato roses, using a sharp knife, pare away skin in a spiral, then coil it round your finger to form a 'rose' shape. To make vandyked tomatoes see page 103.

Serving Suggestions
Thinly sliced tomatoes, sprinkled with olive or walnut oil and chopped basil, make a wonderful side salad; add slices of mozzarella cheese for a delicious first course. Stuff tomatoes with various fillings, such as avocado and crab, taramasalata or herbed cream cheese.

Cooked tomatoes make popular accompaniments: try halved tomatoes topped with garlic-buttered crumbs and a curled anchovy – baked until golden. The large beefsteak type are excellent for stuffing and baking, to serve hot or cold.

Use tomatoes to make soups such as refreshing Gazpacho and tomato and basil soup. Tomatoes make excellent sauces and dips for serving hot and cold. They are of course indispensable in pizza toppings, ratatouille and many fillings for pancakes, pies and quiches. Unripe green tomatoes make marvellous pickles and chutneys.

Beefsteak tomato

Plum (Roma) tomato

Yellow pear tomato

Cherry tomato

Squash

Squash (*Cucurbitaceae*), along with other members of the family such as pumpkin and marrow, are native to the Americas and have been grown for thousands of years. The term squash comes from the American-Indian *askootasquash*.

The squash family is a rather confusing one with squash, pumpkin and marrow being varieties of a single species. To simplify matters, the more well known varieties – namely pumpkin, courgette (zucchini) and vegetable marrow – have individual entries. Most of the other types available can be classified as summer or winter squash.

Summer squash: These are usually thin-skinned, immature and tender and do not need peeling (pumpkin and larger marrows, are exceptions). Summer squash (*Cucurbita pepo*) come in a range of interesting shapes and colours and include the orange, scalloped-shaped **cymling**; light or dark green **patty pan**; pale green pear-shaped **chayote** (choko, or christophene) which contains an edible seed with a nutty flavour; pale green, yellow or white **custard marrow**; and the orange or yellow **crookneck**.

Winter squash: These are more mature and generally larger than summer varieties. They have hard skins, which may or may not be peeled before cooking, according to type and recipe. Varieties of winter squash (*Cucurbita maxima*) include the elongated, pear-shaped yellow **butternut**; dark green **acorn squash**; the large green **hubbard**; the flattish round Japanese **butterball**; and the melon-shaped, yellow **spaghetti squash** (spaghetti marrow). The elongated green **bitter gourd** (*Momordica charantia*) is an Indian squash, albeit from another family.

Buying and Storing

Squash are less familiar in Britain than in other countries, although you will find a variety available throughout the year in specialist shops, ethnic foodshops and large supermarkets. Look for firm squash with unblemished skins.

Summer squash can be stored in the salad drawer of the refrigerator for several days, or longer.

Winter squash keep well for several weeks, or even months, stored in a cool, dry place.

Preparation and Cooking

Trim top and stem ends of summer squash, then leave whole, halve or quarter, slice, dice or cut into chunks, as required. Summer squash may be cooked in the same ways as courgettes (zucchini).

Winter squash are often halved, or cut into wedges, seeded and baked with a tasty filling. They may also be sliced, diced or cut into chunks and steamed, boiled or roasted until tender. Spaghetti marrow is boiled whole in its skin, then halved and the tangled fibres scooped out before serving.

Serving Suggestions

Summer squash are delicious steamed and puréed with butter, cream and seasonings, or served sautéed and sprinkled with finely grated orange rind, cinnamon-flavoured sugar, or crisp crumbled bacon and chives. Enjoy them stuffed and baked with a tasty meat or spiced lentil filling. Or coat slices in batter or egg and crumbs and deep-fry as an unusual accompaniment. Diced summer squash is also good added to casseroles and pot roasts towards the end of cooking. Chayotes are delicious stuffed and baked (see page 92), or try them steamed or boiled until almost tender, then sautéed in garlic butter.

Serve slices of steamed winter squash coated with garlicky tomato sauce and cheese, or dice and add to casseroles and curries. Par-cooked portions of winter squash are good roasted around the joint, or steamed until tender and puréed with butter and spices. Delicious too, in soups, preserves and pickles.

Serve spaghetti marrow hot with melted butter, a rich bolognese sauce, or with cream herbs and cheese. It is also good served cold with vinaigrette.

Butternut

Chayote (choko)

Custard marrow

Acorn squash

Butterball

Spaghetti squash

Bitter gourds

Pumpkin

The pumpkin (*Cucurbita pepo*) has been grown in the Americas for thousands of years; it reached Europe comparatively recently. It is closely related to squash, marrow and courgette (zucchini).

Pumpkins come in a range of shapes with hard, colourful bright orange, green or beige skins; they are all similar in flavour.

Pumpkins are available virtually all year, but especially at Hallowe'en. They are usually rather large, but are often sold cut into smaller pieces. Whole pumpkins store well in a cool, dry place for several weeks; cut portions, covered in plastic wrap, keep successfully in the refrigerator for up to 1 week.

Preparation and Cooking
Pumpkins need cutting into smaller pieces for easy handling. Cut away skin, remove seeds, then slice, dice or cut flesh into chunky pieces, as required. Do not discard the seeds – roasted and salted, they make a delicious snack; good sprinkled over dishes as a garnish, too.

Pumpkin may be steamed, boiled or baked. It may also be steamed in wedges and the flesh scraped away from the skin after cooking.

Serving Suggestions
The most famous use must be American Pumpkin Pie – a tasty mixture of pumpkin purée, spices and cream, served in a pastry case. On the savoury side, pumpkin is excellent puréed in soups, or par-cooked and roasted around the joint – like potatoes. Mashed pumpkin, enriched with butter and flavoured with cinnamon, also makes an unusually good accompaniment. Or try pumpkin diced and sautéed and drizzled with melted butter, honey or maple syrup.

Vegetable Marrow

The vegetable marrow (*Cucurbita pepo ovifera*) is one of the ancient vegetables of the world. It is closely related to the squash, pumpkin and courgette (zucchini).

Marrows are available during summer to early autumn. They vary from light to dark green and/or yellow and are most often striped. Select firm, heavy, smallish marrows as these have plenty of flavour; the large ones can be rather flavourless. Whole marrows will store well in a cool, dry place for as long as a month or so.

Preparation and Cooking
When really young and tender, marrows need not be peeled – simply trim ends top and bottom, cut in pieces and cook as you would courgettes (zucchini). For larger marrows, trim off ends and peel thinly, then slice, cut into halves or rings and remove seeds and surrounding fibres.

Marrow is delicious baked, steamed, braised or sautéed. Take care not to overcook this vegetable or it becomes mushy and tasteless – it is nicest when just tender, but still with a 'bite'.

Serving Suggestions
Stuffed marrow is a great favourite: cut lengthwise in half or into chunky rings, fill with a good flavourful mixture, sprinkle with cheesy crumbs and bake until just tender. Or try chunky pieces of marrow basted and roasted around the joint (add towards the end of cooking time to prevent it over-cooking). Slices of marrow steamed and served in a creamy garlicky sauce make an excellent accompaniment, or bake in a buttered foil parcel (to retain the juices) and sprinkle with fresh herbs just before serving. Diced marrow, sautéed in clarified butter and spiced with a little ground cumin or coriander, is delicious.

Try cream of marrow soup, or perhaps a dish of marrow *au gratin*. Marrow is also an excellent vegetable for making chutneys and delicious marrow and ginger jam.

Pumpkin

Green-striped marrow

Yellow-striped marrow

Spherical Italian courgette (zucchini)

Dark green variety

Yellow courgette (zucchini)

Striped courgette (zucchini)

Courgette (Zucchini)

The courgette (zucchini) (*Cucurbita pepo*) – closely related to squash – is a distinct variety of small vegetable marrow, picked when 10-15 cm (4-6 in) long.

Courgettes (zucchini) are available all year. The skin may be yellow, pale or dark green, or striped. Most varieties are oblong in shape, but a spherical Italian courgette (zucchini) is available.

Buying and Storing

Courgettes (zucchini) are at their best when small. The skin should be smooth and glossy, and the vegetable should feel firm and crisp. Best eaten fresh, although they will keep in the salad drawer of the refrigerator for 2 to 3 days.

Preparation and Cooking

Trim off ends but do not peel. Courgettes (zucchini) can be eaten raw, or cooked whole, sliced or chopped. They may be steamed, sautéed in butter, dipped in batter or egg and breadcrumbs and fried, or stuffed and baked. Take care not to overcook – this vegetable is best when tender, but still crisp.

Serving Suggestions

Diced or thinly sliced raw courgettes (zucchini) are refreshing in salads. Try grated raw courgette (zucchini) and carrot tossed in a herbed French dressing and serve chilled in crisp radicchio cups.

Cut in half, or with a lengthwise slice removed, and partially hollowed out, courgettes (zucchini) are delicious filled with tasty stuffings and served hot or cold. Quartered lengthwise, dipped in a light batter or egg and crumbs and deep-fried, they are very good served hot with a selection of tasty dips, or as an accompaniment to grilled steaks. Delicious too, in ratatouille; served sweet and sour style; or added to stir-fry dishes.

Cucumber

The cucumber (*Cucumis sativus*) was one of the earliest cultivated vegetables, and is thought to be native to India.

There are two basic types of cucumber: the long, thin, smooth-skinned, green hot-house variety; (Continental cucumber); and the rough-skinned, thicker, shorter ridge cucumber – grown outdoors on raised ridges of soil. Mini varieties are available.

Buying and Storing

Available all year round, choose cucumbers that look fresh and feel firm, particularly at the stem end. Store in the salad drawer of the refrigerator for several days (remove tight plastic wrappings).

Ridge cucumbers are better peeled, but only peel the hot-house type if the skin is tough or the cucumber is to be cooked. Cut thin channels in the skin, using a canelle knife, for attractive slices. Cut off ends as these are bitter.

Cucumber is often 'degorged' to remove excess moisture before use (see aubergine (eggplant) page 66).

Serving Suggestions

Cucumber is probably best enjoyed in salads and sandwiches or, cut into sticks, as a crudité for dunking into dips. Hollowed-out cucumber rings, filled with cream cheese, pâté or egg and prawn mayonnaise, are ideal buffet fare. Slices or twists of cucumber make pretty garnishes.

Use cucumber to make pickles and relishes, or grate or dice and mix with yogurt, garlic and perhaps mint, to serve as a refreshing side dish with kebabs and curries.

Cooked cucumber is also good: fill hollowed-out cucumber halves with tasty mixtures, sprinkle with cheese and bake until tender; or cut into cubes or balls, using a melon baller, steam for 15 minutes, then toss in melted butter or thick sour cream; serve as an accompaniment.

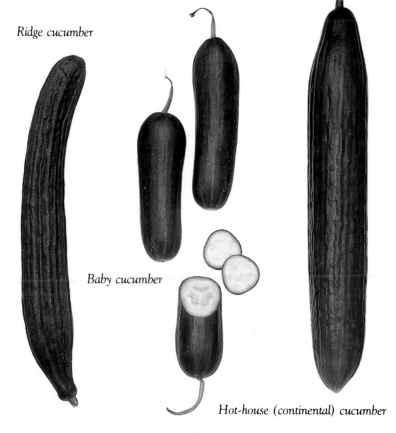

Ridge cucumber

Baby cucumber

Hot-house (continental) cucumber

Aubergine (Eggplant)

The aubergine (eggplant) (*Solanum melongena* var. *esculentum*) is a tropical vegetable fruit native to southern Asia. It is known as *brinjal* in India, *melanzane* in Italy. Aubergines (eggplants) vary in shape – some being long and thin, others pear-shaped or round. Miniature varieties are available. Skin colour varies too – most are purply-black but they can also be yellow or white.

Buying and Storing
Available all year, buy those which are firm, shiny and smooth. They will keep for up to 3 days in the salad drawer of the refrigerator.

Preparation and Cooking
Trim off the leafy end, but do not remove skin. Use a stainless steel knife when preparing to prevent flesh turning black. Slice, chop or dice, or halve and hollow out for stuffing.

As aubergines (eggplants) absorb a lot of oil when fried, they can, be 'degorged' beforehand to reduce this: layer prepared vegetable in a colander with salt, cover with a weighted plate and leave to drain for 30 minutes. Rinse and pat dry.

Aubergines (eggplants) can be baked, stuffed, puréed, grilled, shallow or deep-fried and braised. To fry slices, dust with seasoned flour, then fry in olive oil for 2-3 minutes on each side. To grill slices, brush with oil and grill for 3-4 minutes each side.

To purée for making dips and pâtés, bake at 200C (400F/Gas 6) for 45 minutes or until soft and blackened, then halve and scoop out the flesh.

To stuff an aubergine (eggplant), cut in half lengthwise or cut a slice off one long side. Hollow out the centre, leaving a 2.5 cm (1 in) border. Add the removed flesh (degorged, if wished) to the other filling ingredients, pile back into the shells and bake until tender. Serve hot or cold, depending on filling.

Serving Suggestions
Ratatouille is a favourite – as a starter or accompaniment – or make Ratatouille Cheese Gougère (see page 98). Braised aubergines (eggplants), served with a bowl of thick creamy yogurt, are very good – spice Indian-style if you like.

Use puréed aubergine (eggplant) to make a tasty dip, flavoured with garlic and tahini, and serve with warm pitta bread; or turn into a tasty hot soufflé.

Slices or sticks of aubergine (eggplant), dipped in batter or egg and breadcrumbs and deep-fried, are delicious served hot, sprinkled with grated Parmesan cheese.

Okra

Okra (*Hibiscus esculentus*) came originally from Africa and is now grown in many tropical and subtropical areas. Also known as ladies' fingers, okra is a long, pointed green pod.

Buying and Storing
Okra was once found only in ethnic shops, but it is now more widely available throughout the year. Look for bright, fresh green pods about 10 cm (4 in) long that feel firm and crisp. Avoid any blemished pods. Okra may be stored in a polythene bag in the salad drawer of the refrigerator for 2-3 days.

Preparation and Cooking
Okra may be left whole, sliced or cut into pieces. When cooked for any length of time it secretes a glutinous substance which acts as a thickener for soups and stews. This is essential for the thick Creole-style Gumbo.

Trim okra to remove the stalk, if wished, taking care not to cut off too much of the conical cap or it will become sticky during cooking. Simmer in salted water for 5 minutes until tender-crisp; steam for 10-15 minutes; or sauté in butter or oil for 5-10 minutes, depending on size. Rapid and short cooking is

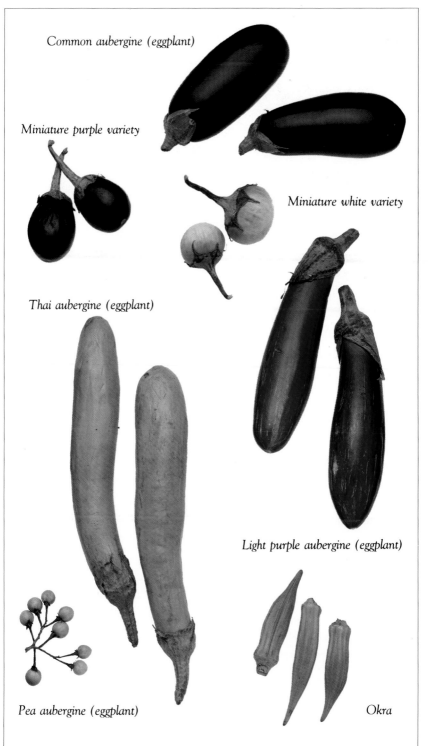

Common aubergine (eggplant)

Miniature purple variety

Miniature white variety

Thai aubergine (eggplant)

Light purple aubergine (eggplant)

Pea aubergine (eggplant)

Okra

best for okra, unless otherwise stated in a recipe, as overcooking causes it to become slimy.

Serving Suggestions
If the pods are very small, they may be sliced and served raw in dressed salads. Okra is delicious sautéed with onions, garlic and tomatoes as an unusual first course. Sprinkled with cheese and buttered crumbs and flashed under a hot grill, it becomes a tasty lunch or supper dish. Try it boiled or steamed and served with lemony butter to eat with the fingers as you would asparagus spears – simple but very good.

As an accompaniment, sauté okra with diced aubergine (eggplant), spiced with onions, garlic, coriander and turmeric; spiced this way it is equally good stirred into hot rice dishes. Okra also makes a delicious and unusual pickle.

Globe artichoke

Young globe artichoke

Globe Artichoke

The globe artichoke (*Cynara scolymus*) originally came from the Mediterranean. Globe artichokes are unopened thistle heads and have no connection with Jerusalem artichokes. Globe artichokes are at their most plentiful during spring and summer. Look out for the very small and immature flower buds, picked before the chokes develop – these are tender enough to be eaten whole.

Buying and Storing
Choose heavy artichokes that feel thick and solid with tightly-packed leaves. Best eaten when fresh, although they will store in a polythene bag in the refrigerator for 2-3 days.

Preparation and Cooking
The small, tender flower buds need only a trim at the stem end and a good washing, to eat. Cook in boiling salted water, or dry white wine flavoured with olive oil and herbs, until just tender; drain and serve hot or cold.

For a large artichoke head, trim stalk level with base and remove any damaged outer leaves. Trim outer leaves, if wished; wash well.

Cook in boiling salted water with a slice of lemon added for 30-45 minutes, until tender. To test, lift from pan and pull off one of the outer leaves – if it comes away easily it is cooked. Drain upside down in a colander. Serve artichoke as it is or with the choke removed (see page 80).

Serving Suggestions
To eat an artichoke, pull off one leaf at a time, dip the tender succulent end into a sauce and nibble off the soft fleshy part with your teeth. Discard the rest of the leaf (provide finger bowls and plates for discarded leaves). The heart is then eaten with a knife and fork, provided the choke has been removed.

Serve artichokes hot with melted butter, lemon butter or hollandaise, or cold with vinaigrette, *aïoli* or a rich garlicky tomato sauce. Served cold, they are also extremely good filled with a pâté or seafood mixture.

Artichoke hearts are excellent blanched and sautéed in butter or dipped in egg and breadcrumbs and deep-fried. They are delicious, too, added to salads.

Sweetcorn

Sweetcorn (*Zea mays*), also known as Indian corn, is a type of maize native to Central America, where it has been grown for over 5,000 years. It was introduced to Europe in the 16th century.

Corn-on-the-cob is available during summer and autumn. Dwarf (baby) corns are in the shops more or less all year.

Buying and Storing
Select cobs that are full and plump with bright creamy coloured kernels – not dark yellow as this is a sign of age. If fresh and tender, a kernel of corn exudes a milky liquid when split open. Eat corn cobs fresh or keep for 1-2 days, wrapped in a polythene bag in the refrigerator. Dwarf corns keep well in the salad drawer of the refrigerator for several days.

Preparation and Cooking
Trim away outer leaves, silky threads and stalks from corn cobs and wash thoroughly. Cook in boiling *unsalted* water for 5-8 minutes for freshly-picked corn; 15-20 minutes if older. Add a pinch of sugar to the pan, if wished. Salt and overcooking both toughen corn.

Corn cobs may also be grilled or barbecued for 8-10 minutes, brushed liberally with butter and turned frequently; if the cobs are older, boil for 10 minutes first. Alternatively, brush corn cobs with butter, wrap in foil and bake at 180C (350F/Gas 4) for 30 minutes.

To remove the kernels from the cob, hold the cob firmly, stalk end down on a flat surface and, using a sharp knife, make downward strokes, to cut away the kernels. Cook these in boiling *unsalted* water for 6-8 minutes, or steam for 10-15 minutes.

Dwarf corn may be eaten raw or cooked. Simply wash and serve raw, or boil, steam or stir-fry briefly until tender-crisp.

Serving Suggestions
Very fresh, tender young kernels are delicious added raw to salads or use dwarf corn cobs as dipping sticks with *aïoli*. Stir kernels into a thick batter and fry to make fritters. Make into a creamy soup or add to a thick, chunky fish chowder. Mix kernels into stir-fry dishes, savoury rice and pasta dishes.

Whole corn cobs are best served with plenty of melted butter and freshly ground black pepper. Par-cooked corn cobs, cut into chunky slices, make an attractive addition to kebabs.

Corn-on-the-cob

Dwarf (baby) corn

Avocado

Fuerte

The avocado is actually a fruit (belonging to the genus *Persea*). It is included here because it is more often served as a vegetable. For centuries it has been cultivated and eaten in its native South America; indeed, its name is derived from the aztec *ahuacet*. Avocados are now grown in most tropical countries and are popular worldwide. Believe it or not, there are over 500 varieties of avocado.

The most popular varieties are **Ettinger,** oblong with bright, shiny, smooth green skin; **Hass,** a purply black-skinned variety; **Fuerte,** oblong with dark green, slightly rough skin; and **Habal,** a large round fruit with a large stone. There is also now a tiny **Cocktail** avocado available which has no stone.

Buying and Storing

Avocados are in the shops all year round. To enjoy them, they must be perfectly ripe. You can't assess ripeness by looking at the skin, so cradle the fruit in the palm of your hand – it should yield slightly all over to gentle pressure. Store ripe avocados in the salad drawer of the refrigerator for up to 3 days. Cut avocados, sprinkled with lemon juice and with their stone still in, keep for up to 24 hours, wrapped in plastic wrap in the refrigerator.

To speed up ripening, place un-ripe avocados in a fruit bowl with bananas in a warm room.

Preparation

To open an avocado, cut in half lengthwise through to the stone, using a stainless steel knife, then separate into halves by carefully rotating each portion in opposite directions. Remove stone and rub cut surfaces with lemon juice to prevent discoloration. To slice, if required, peel off skin, place cut side down and slice lengthwise, or crosswise if preferred.

Serving Suggestions

As starters, avocados are always popular halved, stoned and filled with a vinaigrette or prawn mixture. For a change, fill the cavities with Roquefort mayonnaise or flaked crabmeat marinated in lemon juice. Avocado and grapefruit slices complement each other perfectly as a delicate first course.

Puréed avocado flesh makes a refreshing and stylish chilled soup, and delicious dips, such as spicy Mexican Guacamole.

The nutty, delicate flavour and succulent texture of avocados makes them ideal to include in salads: try avocado with bacon and spinach, or chicken and avocado salad.

Avocados may also be baked with a savoury filling – a creamy seafood mixture is particularly good – though some folk claim that the delicate flavour of avocado is not as good hot.

Habal

Hass

Sharwil

Cocktail avocado

Pepper

There are many varieties of pepper, but the two important species are the sweet pepper (*Capsicum annuum*) and the chilli pepper (*Capsicum frutescens*). Both are native to the West Indies and tropical America.

SWEET PEPPER

Sweet peppers come in a range of colours and sizes. The crisp green pepper is the unripe fruit which, as it matures, turns red or yellow (according to variety). White, brown and purple/black peppers are also available, but not as widely as the green, yellow and red types.

Flavour and texture of the various coloured peppers varies slightly: green are crisp and mildly spicy; yellow ones are crisp and slightly sweeter; red peppers are softer in texture with the sweetest flavour of all. The white and purple/black varieties are similar to green peppers. The bell-shaped Scotch bonnets are spicy.

It is the red pepper which is dried and ground to make paprika. Canned red peppers are called pimentos.

CHILLI PEPPER

The chilli pepper is much smaller than the sweet pepper and is generally used as a flavouring rather than a vegetable. Chillies vary in size, shape and heat factor according to ripeness – but they are always hot and fiery, so be warned!

Fresh chillies are available green, yellow or red: generally the smaller the variety the hotter they seem to be. Red chillies are usually sweeter and more mellow in flavour than the green ones; yellow chillies are similar in flavour to the red kind.

Dried chillies are ground to make hot cayenne pepper and, combined with other spices, are used to make chilli and curry powders. Chillies are also available canned in brine, and dried – whole or in flakes.

Buying and Storing

Peppers and chillies are available all year: select those that feel firm and have smooth glossy skins. They will keep well in the salad drawer of the refrigerator for up to 1 week.

Preparation

Cut off stalk ends of peppers and discard seeds and pith. Peppers for stuffing may be blanched in boiling water for 5 minutes to make them pliable and reduce baking time.

To skin peppers: grill or bake whole until the skin blisters and blackens, then peel of the thin skin and discard – this also makes peppers more digestible.

Peppers may be sliced, diced or cut into larger pieces, according to requirement. They are delicious sautéed, braised, stewed, steamed or baked.

When preparing chillies take great care as the seeds and juices cause skin irritation. Wear rubber gloves when handling chillies and be sure not to touch your face or eyes during preparation. Cut off stalk end and split open pods. The tiny cream-coloured seeds inside the pods are the hottest part and are usually removed before using: carefully scrape them out using a pointed knife and discard. Rinse pods very thoroughly under cold running water and pat dry. Chop finely or cut into thin slivers before using. When preparation is complete, wash hands, utensils and work surface thoroughly.

Serving Suggestions

Peppers are delicious eaten raw or cooked. Enjoy them crisp, juicy and raw in salads, or use as 'dipping sticks' for hummous and taramasalata. Fill whole peppers with pâtés and cream cheese mixtures, then chill and slice into rings to serve as starters.

Use peppers in piperade, ratatouille and peperonata; add to soups, sauces and stir-fry dishes; or use to add 'bite' to pickles, chutney and relishes.

Chillies add pungency to many dishes, but remember that a little goes a long way. Steep a whole chilli in a jar of oil and use the flavoured oil in salad dressings, marinades and for sautéeing. Add shredded chilli to Chinese and Indian dishes, pizza toppings, omelettes and scrambled egg.

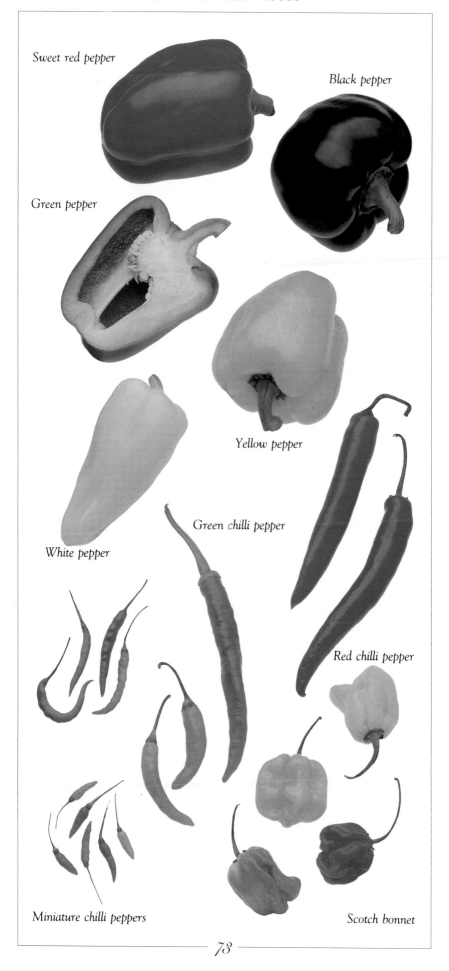

Sweet red pepper

Black pepper

Green pepper

Yellow pepper

White pepper

Green chilli pepper

Red chilli pepper

Miniature chilli peppers

Scotch bonnet

Iced Avocado Soup

3 teaspoons sunflower oil
6 spring onions, thinly sliced
4 teaspoons plain flour
470 ml (15 fl oz/1¾ cups) chicken stock
2 ripe avocados
2 teaspoons lemon juice
470 ml (15 fl oz/1¾ cups) milk
155 ml (5 fl oz/⅔ cup) thick sour cream
salt and white pepper, to taste
2 good pinches cayenne pepper
TO GARNISH:
4 teaspoons thick sour cream
chives

1 In a saucepan, heat oil, add spring onions and fry gently for 2 minutes, stirring frequently. Stir in flour and cook for 1 minute, then gradually stir in stock and bring to the boil, stirring. Reduce heat and simmer gently for 10 minutes. Leave to cool.

2 Cut avocados in half, peel and remove stones. Slice off a little for garnishing, brush with 1 teaspoon lemon juice and set aside. Cut up remaining avocados, put in a blender or food processor with the cooled sauce mixture and blend until smooth.

3 Add milk, thick sour cream and remaining lemon juice and blend thoroughly to combine. Season with salt, white pepper and cayenne and mix well. Chill for at least 2 hours before serving.

Pour into 4 individual serving bowls and garnish each with a teaspoon of sour cream, slivers of avocado, and a few chives.

Serves 4.

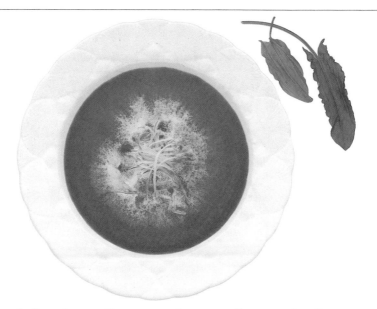

Nettle, Spinach & Sorrel Soup

90 g (3 oz) tender young nettle tops
a good handful of small sorrel leaves
185 g (6 oz) spinach leaves
45 g (1½ oz) butter
1 Spanish onion, thinly sliced
1 large potato, about 250 g (8 oz), peeled and diced
470 ml (15 fl oz/1¾ cups) chicken stock
220 ml (7 fl oz/1 cup) creamy milk
5 tablespoons single (light) cream
salt and pepper, to taste
TO GARNISH:
a little double (thick) cream
45 g (1½ oz/⅓ cup) grated Gruyère cheese

1 Pick over nettle tops and sorrel, removing sorrel stalks. Remove stalks from spinach. Rinse vegetables well in several changes of cold water. Shake well to drain, then shred coarsely.

2 In a large saucepan, melt butter, add shredded vegetables, onion and potato and fry gently for 10 minutes, shaking pan frequently. Stir in stock, bring to the boil, then cover and simmer for 20 minutes, until potato and onion are tender.

3 Purée mixture in a blender or food processor until smooth. Return to pan and stir in milk and cream. Add seasoning and reheat gently. Pour into 4 individual warmed soup bowls and garnish with a swirl of cream and a sprinkling of grated cheese. Serve hot.

Serves 4.

Note: Do wear rubber gloves when preparing nettles.

Spiced Pumpkin Soup

750 g (1½ lb) pumpkin
2.5 cm (1 in) piece fresh root (green) ginger
30 g (1 oz) butter
1 large Spanish onion, chopped
¼ teaspoon garam masala
3 teaspoons plain flour
625 ml (20 fl oz/2½ cups) chicken stock
salt and pepper, to taste
1 tablespoon snipped chives
1 tablespoon chopped coriander
60 ml (2 fl oz/¼ cup) single (light) cream
TO GARNISH:
sprigs of coriander

1 Cut unpeeled pumpkin into even pieces; cut away seeds. Put in a steamer, cover and steam for about 30 minutes or until tender. Leave to cool slightly, then scrape away flesh from skin and mash well or purée in a blender or food processor.

2 Peel ginger and chop very finely. In a saucepan, melt butter, add onion and fry gently for 5 minutes; stir in ginger and garam masala and cook for 2 minutes, stirring. Add flour and cook for 1 minute. Gradually stir in stock and bring to the boil, stirring. Reduce heat, then add pumpkin and seasoning.

3 Cover and simmer gently for 10 minutes. Stir in herbs and cream. Remove from heat and adjust seasoning, if necessary. Serve hot, garnished with coriander.

Serves 4-6.

Note: Vegetable stock may be used instead of chicken stock, if preferred.

This soup is also good served garnished with toasted pumpkin seeds or a little finely grated Cheddar cheese.

Broad Bean Soup Gratinée

3 teaspoons olive oil
45 g (1½ oz) butter
1 clove garlic, crushed
1 Spanish onion, halved and sliced
3 large lettuce leaves, shredded
3 teaspoons plain flour
625 ml (20 fl oz/2½ cups) chicken stock
500 g (1 lb) shelled broad beans
salt and pepper, to taste
4 slices French bread, about 2.5 cm (1 in) thick
1½ teaspoons Dijon mustard
125 g (4 oz/1 cup) grated Gruyère cheese
TO GARNISH:
snipped chives

1 In a saucepan, heat the oil and 30 g (1 oz) butter. Add garlic, onion and lettuce and fry gently for 3 minutes, stirring frequently. Stir in flour and cook for 1 minute. Stir in 315 ml (10 fl oz/1¼ cups) stock and bring to the boil, stirring. Reduce heat, add broad beans, cover and simmer for 25 minutes.

2 Transfer half the mixture to a blender or food processor and blend until smooth; return to pan. Repeat with remaining mixture. Stir in remaining stock and seasoning. Reheat, stirring, until piping hot. Transfer to 4 individual flameproof soup bowls and place in grill pan. Preheat grill.

3 Spread French bread with remaining butter and mustard and press down into soup. Sprinkle with cheese and cook under moderate grill for 6-8 minutes, until golden and melted. Sprinkle with chives and serve immediately.

Serves 4.

Note: For a chunky soup, purée half of the mixture only in step 2. For a thinner soup, add a little extra stock.

Crudités with Skorthalia

90 g (3 oz) slightly stale white bread, crusts removed
2-3 cloves garlic, crushed
3 teaspoons white wine vinegar
½ teaspoon each salt and pepper
90 ml (3 fl oz/⅓ cup) olive oil
3 teaspoons lemon juice
30 g (1 oz/¼ cup) ground almonds
3 teaspoons chopped mint
1 head of chicory (Belgian endive)
1 red pepper
2 courgettes (zucchini)
2 sticks celery
12 radishes
¼ cauliflower
1 black olive, cut into slivers
sprig of mint

1 Cut bread into cubes and put into a bowl. Add enough cold water just to cover; leave to soak for 5 minutes. Turn into a sieve and, using a wooden spoon, press bread against sieve to extract water. Put bread into a blender or food processor with garlic, vinegar and salt and pepper. Blend until smooth.

2 With motor running, gradually add olive oil, in a thin stream, and blend until completely absorbed. Blend in lemon juice, ground almonds and mint; adjust seasoning, if necessary. Turn into a serving bowl and chill for at least 1 hour.

3 Prepare crudités: divide chicory (Belgian endive) into separate leaves; cut red pepper into strips; slice courgettes (zucchini) lengthwise, then cut into sticks; cut celery into small sticks; discard leaves from radishes and trim base ends; break cauliflower into bite-sized flowerets. Wash all vegetables, drain and pat dry on absorbent kitchen paper. Chill until required.

Put dip in the centre of a large serving platter. Arrange prepared vegetables in groups around bowl. Garnish dip with olives and mint.

Serves 4-6.

Salmon & Guacamole Terrine

15 g (½ oz) butter
15 g (½ oz/6 teaspoons) plain flour
213 g (7 oz) can salmon
5 teaspoons lemon juice
4½ teaspoons powdered gelatine
5 tablespoons mayonnaise
4 teaspoons tomato purée (paste)
60 ml (2 fl oz/¼ cup) double (thick) cream
few drops of Worcestershire sauce
salt and pepper, to taste
2 ripe avocados
1 clove garlic, crushed
1 teaspoon olive oil
2 pinches of cayenne pepper
TO GARNISH:
sprigs of dill

1 In a saucepan, melt butter, add flour and cook for 1 minute. Drain salmon, reserving liquor; make up to 185 ml (6 fl oz/¾ cup) with water. Stir liquor into pan and bring to the boil, stirring; cook for 2 minutes. Remove from heat. Flake salmon finely; stir into sauce.

In a bowl, mix 3 teaspoons lemon juice and 6 teaspoons water; sprinkle over gelatine and leave for 5 minutes. Stand bowl in a pan of hot water; stir until dissolved. Leave until cool but not set.

2 Add 4 tablespoons mayonnaise, tomato purée (paste), cream and Worcestershire sauce to salmon mixture; season and mix well. Stir in gelatine; chill for 15 minutes. Peel, stone and thinly slice 1 avocado; brush with 1 teaspoon lemon juice. One-third fill a dampened 500 g (1 lb) loaf tin with salmon mixture. Cover with half the avocado; repeat layers, finishing with salmon. Chill for at least 2 hours.

3 Peel, stone and mash remaining avocado in a bowl. Add remaining lemon juice and mayonnaise, garlic, oil, cayenne and salt. Chill.

Dip terrine into very hot water for 2-3 seconds, then turn out onto a serving plate. Swirl guacamole sauce over top. Garnish with dill.

Serves 6-8.

Globe Artichokes à la Grecque

4 large globe artichokes
SAUCE:
2 tablespoons tomato purée (paste)
4 tablespoons olive oil
155 ml (5 fl oz/⅔ cup) dry white wine
1 small onion, finely chopped
1 clove garlic, crushed
1 teaspoon chopped oregano
2 sprigs of thyme
2 ripe tomatoes, skinned and chopped
salt and pepper, to taste
TO GARNISH:
lemon wedges
sprigs of oregano

1 Cut off stalks from artichokes and, using scissors, trim off pointed ends from outer leaves. Rinse well. Cook in boiling salted water for 15 minutes. Drain well and leave upside down on absorbent kitchen paper to dry.

2 To make sauce, put all the ingredients into a saucepan, add 155 ml (5 fl oz/⅔ cup) cold water, mix well and bring to the boil, then cover and simmer gently for 10 minutes, stirring occasionally. Remove thyme sprigs. Add par-cooked artichokes to sauce, cover and cook gently for 30 minutes Carefully lift artichokes onto a plate and leave to cool. Boil sauce, uncovered, for 5 minutes; leave to cool.

3 When artichokes are cold, remove chokes by spreading top leaves apart and pulling out the inside leaves to reveal the hairy choke. Using a teaspoon, scrape away hairs to expose the heart. Arrange artichokes on 4 individual serving plates and spoon sauce around base. Cover and chill until required.

Garnish with lemon wedges and oregano to serve.

Serves 4.

Sesame-glazed Asparagus

500 g (1 lb) asparagus
60 g (2 oz) butter
6 spring onions, thinly sliced diagonally
finely grated rind of ½ small lemon
1 tablespoon lemon juice
salt and pepper, to taste
pinch of cayenne pepper
1-2 tablespoons sesame seeds, lightly toasted
1 teaspoon sesame oil
TO GARNISH:
lemon slices
sprigs of flat-leaf parsley

1 Cut off woody part at base of asparagus stems and, using a knife, scrape off white part of stems. Cut asparagus spears diagonally into 3 or 4 equal pieces. Put into a saucepan and add enough boiling salted water to cover. Cook, covered, for 8-10 minutes, until just tender; drain well.

2 In a large frying pan, melt butter, then add spring onions and fry gently for 1 minute. Add lemon rind and juice, then stir in asparagus; toss lightly in the sauce over a gentle heat for 2-3 minutes, until heated through.

3 Season with salt, pepper and cayenne. Turn onto a warmed serving platter and sprinkle with toasted sesame seeds and sesame oil. Garnish with lemon slices and parsley; serve hot.

Serves 4.

Parma & Asparagus Parcels

16 asparagus spears
4 slices Parma ham (prosciutto), halved lengthwise
8 long chives
a little lemon juice for sprinkling
freshly ground black pepper
HOLLANDAISE SAUCE:
60 ml (2 fl oz/¼ cup) white wine vinegar
1 teaspoon black peppercorns
2 large egg yolks
125 g (4 oz) butter, at room temperature
2-3 pinches of cayenne pepper
TO GARNISH:
lemon twists

1 Cut off woody base of asparagus stems and, using a knife, scrape off white part of stems. Tie asparagus in bundles with heads together; put in an asparagus steamer or saucepan and add enough boiling water to reach just below asparagus heads. Cover and boil for 12-14 minutes or until tender. Lift asparagus from water, drain and set aside.

2 To make Hollandaise sauce, put vinegar and peppercorns in a saucepan, bring to the boil and boil until reduced by half. Put egg yolks in a bowl with 15 g (½ oz) butter and beat well. Strain hot vinegar onto the butter, beating well. Return to pan and put over very low heat.

Gradually add remaining butter in small pieces, whisking constantly until sauce is thickened and smooth. (Take care at this stage: keep removing pan from heat whilst beating in butter to prevent curdling.) Add cayenne and transfer to a serving dish.

3 Cut asparagus spears in half. Form 4 pieces into a stack, with spear ends on top. Wrap in a piece of ham and tie with a chive. Repeat with remaining asparagus, ham and chives. Sprinkle with lemon juice and pepper, garnish with lemon and serve with Hollandaise.

Serves 4.

Wafer-wrapped Vegetables

3 spring onions, finely chopped
90 g (3 oz) Chinese cabbage, finely chopped
½ red or green pepper, finely chopped
1 clove garlic, crushed
125 g (4 oz) peeled prawns, thawed if frozen, chopped
3 teaspoons light soy sauce
3 teaspoons oyster sauce
½ teaspoon caster sugar
1 teaspoon cornflour
4 sheets filo pastry
vegetable oil for deep-frying
TO SERVE:
spring onion flowers (see page 43)
chilli sauce

1 In a small saucepan, mix together spring onions, Chinese cabbage, red or green pepper, garlic and prawns. Stir in soy sauce, oyster sauce, sugar and cornflour. Cook over a medium heat for 3 minutes, stirring constantly. Remove from heat; set aside.

2 Cut sheets of filo pastry into twenty-four 13 cm (5 in) squares. Sandwich together in pairs to form 12 double-thickness squares. Put a teaspoon of prepared mixture in the centre of each square, then draw the corners of the pastry together, twist and pinch firmly to seal and form neat bags.

3 Half-fill a deep pan with oil and heat to 190C (375F) or until a cube of day-old bread browns in 40 seconds. Lower vegetable bags into oil, a few at a time, and deep-fry for 2-3 minutes, until golden brown; drain on absorbent kitchen paper and keep warm while cooking remainder. Arrange on a warm serving plate and garnish with spring onion flowers. Serve hot with a bowl of chilli sauce for 'dipping'.

Serves 4-6.

Variation: Omit prawns and add cooked, minced pork instead.

Plaice & Watercress Filos

2 plaice fillets, skinned and boned
1½ bunches watercress
90 g (3 oz) butter
3 shallots, finely chopped
1 tablespoon fresh lime juice
salt and pepper, to taste
5 sheets filo pastry
TO SERVE:
watercress sprigs
lime twists
tartare sauce

1 Preheat oven to 190C (375F/Gas 5). Cut plaice fillets into thin strips and place in a bowl. Trim off watercress stalks and coarsely chop the leaves. In a saucepan, melt 30 g (1 oz) butter, add watercress and shallots and cook very gently for 2 minutes; transfer to the bowl. Add lime juice and seasoning. Mix well and set aside.

2 Melt remaining butter in a pan. Cut filo sheets in half crosswise; brush lightly with butter. Fold each piece into 3 layers by folding top one-third section over centre one-third and bottom one-third over top to form a long narrow strip. Brush lightly with butter. Divide filling into 10 portions; put one in a corner of each pastry strip.

3 Fold pastry and filling over at right angles to form a triangle. Continue folding in this way along strip of pastry to form neat triangular parcels. Brush all over with remaining melted butter and put on a baking sheet. Cook in the oven for 15 minutes, until golden brown and cooked through.

Serve hot, garnished with watercress and lime twists. Accompany with tartare sauce.

Makes 10.

Japanese-style Cucumber

1 cucumber
1 bunch watercress, stalks trimmed
125 g (4 oz) white crabmeat, fresh or frozen
and thawed
2.5 cm (1 in) piece fresh root (green) ginger, peeled
and grated
salt and pepper, to taste
SAUCE:
2 tablespoons rice vinegar or distilled malt vinegar
2 tablespoons chicken stock
2 teaspoons caster sugar
2 teaspoons Japanese soy sauce
TO GARNISH:
watercress sprigs

1 Trim ends of cucumber, then slit lengthwise along one side through to centre; take care not to cut right through. Using a teaspoon, very carefully remove seedy flesh from centre to form a channel.

Blanch watercress in boiling water for 30 seconds; drain well and pat dry on absorbent kitchen paper.

2 In a bowl, finely flake crabmeat; add ginger and seasoning. Hold cut edges of cucumber open and carefully insert crab mixture into channel; top with blanched watercress.

Press cucumber edges together and wrap tightly in plastic wrap. Chill for at least 2 hours.

3 To make the sauce, put all the ingredients into a small saucepan and bring to the boil, stirring. Remove from heat and leave to cool.

Just before serving, cut cucumber into 2 cm (¾ in) thick slices and arrange on a flat serving platter. Pour a little sauce over each slice and garnish with watercress.

Serves 4-6.

Spinach & Anchovy Soufflé

500 g (1 lb) spinach
60 g (2 oz) butter
60 g (2 oz/½ cup) plain flour
315 ml (10 fl oz/1¼ cups) milk
3 large egg yolks
60 g (2 oz/½ cup) grated Cheddar cheese
5 canned anchovy fillets, drained and finely
chopped
pepper, to taste
freshly grated nutmeg
4 large egg whites
TO GARNISH:
cherry tomatoes

1 Discard tough stalks from washed spinach; shake off excess moisture. Pack into a saucepan (without additional water), cover and cook gently, turning occasionally, until volume decreases, then simmer for 8-10 minutes, until tender. Turn into a sieve and press with a saucer to extract moisture. Chop finely in a food processor.

2 Preheat oven to 180C (350F/Gas 4). Lightly grease a 1.2 litre (40 fl oz/5 cup) soufflé dish. In a saucepan, melt butter, stir in flour and cook for 1 minute; add milk and bring to the boil, stirring. Reduce heat and simmer for 2 minutes, stirring. Remove from heat and mix in spinach, egg yolks, cheese and anchovies. Season with pepper and nutmeg. Whisk egg whites until soft peaks form; add 3 tablespoons to spinach mixture and stir to mix. Using a large metal spoon, lightly fold in remaining egg white.

3 Pour mixture into prepared soufflé dish and smooth surface. Run the back of a metal spoon around outer edge to form a central dome (for the 'top hat' effect). Cook in the oven for 40-45 minutes, until well risen and golden brown. Serve immediately, garnished with cherry tomatoes.

Serves 3-4.

Chicken Szechuan

500 g (1 lb) skinned chicken breast fillets
4 carrots
1 large red pepper, cored and seeded
6 spring onions
4 cm (1½ in) piece fresh root (green) ginger
2 large eggs, beaten
salt and pepper, to taste
125 g (4 oz/1 cup) cornflour
oil for frying
1 clove garlic, crushed
4 teaspoons caster sugar
2 tablespoons soy sauce
2 tablespoons malt vinegar
TO GARNISH:
sprigs of chervil

1 Slice chicken into thin strips. Cut carrots and red pepper into matchstick strips. Cut spring onions into 3 equal pieces, then cut into slivers. Peel ginger and slice thinly, then cut into slivers.

In a bowl, mix eggs with salt and pepper. Dip chicken strips into egg, then into cornflour to coat.

2 In a large saucepan, heat a 5 cm (2 in) depth of oil. Add a quarter of the chicken strips and fry for 3-4 minutes, until cooked through and lightly golden; drain on absorbent kitchen paper while cooking remainder in batches.

In a wok or frying pan, heat 3 tablespoons oil, add carrot and red pepper strips and stir-fry for 1½ minutes. Remove with a slotted spoon and set aside. Add garlic and ginger to pan and stir-fry for 30 seconds.

3 Add sugar, soy sauce and vinegar to wok. Return vegetables to wok, add chicken and toss in the sauce for 2-3 minutes to heat through and glaze. Add spring onion slivers and toss lightly. Serve immediately, garnished with chervil.

Serves 4.

Note: This dish is delicious served with plain boiled rice and accompanied by prawn crackers.

Scampi Mediterranean

4 ripe tomatoes
1 Spanish onion
2 courgettes (zucchini)
1 red pepper, cored and seeded
4 tablespoons olive oil
1 clove garlic, crushed
15 g (½ oz/6 teaspoons) plain flour
60 ml (2 fl oz/¼ cup) dry white wine
1 tablespoon tomato purée (paste)
salt and pepper, to taste
500 g (1 lb) raw, peeled scampi
45 g (1½ oz/¾ cup) fresh white breadcrumbs
3 teaspoons chopped marjoram
125 g (4 oz) mozzarella cheese
TO GARNISH:
sprigs of marjoram

1 Preheat oven to 190C (375F/Gas 5). Put tomatoes in a bowl, cover with boiling water and leave for 30 seconds; drain and peel away skins, then chop coarsely. Quarter and thinly slice onion. Cut courgettes (zucchini) into 5 mm (¼ in) slices. Cut red pepper into fairly thin strips.

In a saucepan, heat 3 tablespoons oil, add garlic, onion, courgettes (zucchini) and red pepper and cook gently for 3 minutes. 2 Stir in flour and cook for 1 minute. Add wine, tomato purée (paste) and 220 ml (7 fl oz/1 cup) water. Season with salt and pepper and cook gently for 5 minutes, stirring occasionally. Add tomatoes and mix well. Divide mixture between 4 individual ovenproof dishes. Top with scampi.

3 Heat remaining oil in a pan. Remove from heat and stir in breadcrumbs and marjoram; mix well. Sprinkle over mixture in dishes. Chop mozzarella cheese and sprinkle on top. Cook in the oven for 30 minutes or until the topping is golden and the scampi is cooked. Serve hot, garnished with sprigs of marjoram.

Serves 4.

Tempura

1 courgette (zucchini)
1 small aubergine (eggplant)
1 green pepper, cored and seeded
8 button mushrooms, trimmed
2 small sweet potatoes, peeled
6 spring onions
2 lemon sole or plaice fillets, skinned and boned
4 cooked King prawns in shell
vegetable oil for deep-frying
1 egg yolk
250 g (8 oz/2 cups) plain flour
½ teaspoon bicarbonate of soda
DIPPING SAUCE:
3 tablespoons mirin (Japanese rice wine)
3 tablespoons Japanese soy sauce
315 ml (10 fl oz/1¼ cups) chicken stock

1 Cut courgette (zucchini) and aubergine (eggplant) into 1 cm (½ in) slices. Halve aubergine (eggplant) slices. Cut green pepper into 2.5 cm (1 in) pieces. Cut sweet potatoes into 5 mm (¼ in) slices. Cut spring onions and fish into bite-size pieces.

2 Peel prawns, except for the last segment of the tail shells.

To make batter, mix egg yolk and 470 ml (15 fl oz/1¾ cups) ice cold water in a jug. Sift flour and bicarbonate of soda into a bowl and gradually add liquid, whisking until smooth. Let stand for 15 minutes.

To make dipping sauce, put mirin, soy sauce and stock into a pan and bring to the boil. Let cool.

3 Half-fill a wok or deep pan with vegetable oil and heat to 190C (375F) or until a cube of day-old bread browns in 40 seconds. Dip pieces of vegetable and fish, a few at a time, into batter, then deep-fry for 1-2 minutes, until lightly golden. Drain well and keep warm while cooking remainder.

Put a bowl of dipping sauce on each warmed serving plate and surround with vegetables and fish.

Serves 4.

Note: If mirin is unavailable, substitute medium sherry.

Eastern-style Hotpot

1.75 litres (3 pints/7½ cups) chicken stock
2.5 cm (1 in) piece fresh root (green) ginger, peeled and grated
1 clove garlic, crushed
1 skinned chicken breast fillet
185 g (6 oz) rump or fillet steak
60 g (2 oz) mange tout (snow peas)
2 courgettes (zucchini)
½ Chinese cabbage
1 bunch spring onions
DIPPING SAUCE:
½ teaspoon chilli sauce
1 clove garlic, crushed
4 tablespoons light soy sauce
2 tablespoons peanut oil
good pinch of caster sugar
1 teaspoon vinegar

1 In a saucepan, put stock, ginger and garlic; cover and simmer for 10 minutes. Meanwhile, cut chicken and steak into very thin strips.
2 Top and tail mange tout (snow peas) and remove strings. Slice courgettes (zucchini) thinly. Cut Chinese cabbage and spring onions into short lengths. Arrange vegetables, chicken and steak on a serving platter.

To make dipping sauce, mix all ingredients together; transfer to small serving bowls.

Transfer stock mixture to a Mongolian hotpot or large metal fondue pot over a burner in the centre of the table; bring back to simmering.
3 Guests cook their own meal at the table: hold pieces of chicken or steak and one or two vegetables in small Chinese wire baskets and lower into the simmering stock to cook for 1½-2 minutes. (Alternatively, hold the food with wooden chopsticks in the stock.) Dip into the dipping sauce before eating. Continue until the ingredients are used up. Serve the remaining stock in soup bowls.

Serves 4.

Braised Veal Turnips

8 turnips, about 125 g (4 oz) each, peeled
155 g (5 oz) butter
1 onion, finely chopped
375 g (12 oz) veal escalope, minced
finely grated rind of 1 large lemon
125 g (4 oz/2 cups) fresh breadcrumbs
8 sage leaves, finely chopped
4 tablespoons chopped parsley
1 large egg, beaten
salt and pepper, to taste
315 ml (10 fl oz/1¼ cups) chicken stock
8 tablespoons double (thick) cream
8 slices beefsteak tomato, about 1 cm (½ in) thick
TO GARNISH:
sprigs of parsley and sage

1 In a saucepan of boiling salted water, cook the turnips for 15-20 minutes or until tender when pierced with a skewer. Drain and leave until cool enough to handle. Hollow out turnips, using a melon baller or teaspoon, leaving a 5 mm (¼ in) shell.

2 Preheat oven to 180C (350F/Gas 4). In a frying pan, melt 125 g (4 oz) butter, add onion and veal and cook for 5 minutes, stirring. Remove from heat, stir in lemon rind, breadcrumbs, half the sage and parsley, beaten egg and salt and pepper; mix well. Spoon into hollowed-out turnips and pile up to cover top surface area completely; press into neat mounds. Put in a greased shallow ovenproof dish. Melt remaining butter and brush over stuffing and turnips; add 8 tablespoons stock to dish. Cook in the oven for 40 minutes, until stuffing is golden. Transfer turnips to a plate; keep warm.

3 Pour juices from dish into a pan. Add remaining stock and herbs, and cream; simmer for 4-5 minutes, until slightly thickened. Put tomato slices on a warmed serving dish, place a halved turnip on each and spoon over the sauce. Garnish with parsley and sage to serve.

Serves 4.

Chillied Pork Chayotes

4 large chayotes
2 tablespoons olive oil
1 onion, chopped
1 clove garlic, crushed
250 g (8 oz) lean pork, minced
1 fresh green chilli, seeded and finely chopped
4 tomatoes, skinned and chopped
2 tablespoons tomato purée (paste)
1 teaspoon cumin seeds
1 teaspoon hot chilli powder
90 g (3 oz/¾ cup) grated Cheddar cheese
4 grissini (bread sticks), crushed
TO GARNISH:
4 tablespoons thick sour cream
sprigs of thyme
4 pickled chillies (optional)

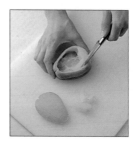

1 Cook chayotes in boiling salted water for 30 minutes or until tender (test by inserting a skewer through the skins); drain and cool under running cold water. Set aside.

Preheat oven to 190C (375F/Gas 5). In a saucepan, heat oil, add onion, garlic, pork and chilli and fry gently for 5 minutes, stirring frequently. Stir in tomatoes, tomato purée (paste), cumin, chilli powder and 4 tablespoons cold water, cover and cook gently for 5 minutes. Uncover and cook for 5 minutes, until thickened.

2 Cut a sliver off one long side of each chayote to sit level. Slice off the top one-third of each; cut out flesh and seeds, leaving a 5 mm (¼ in) border. Drain upside down on absorbent kitchen paper. Drain and chop flesh and seeds. Add to pork mixture with half the cheese and crushed grissini; mix well.

3 Spoon mixture into prepared chayote shells, piling it up neatly on top; put into a greased shallow ovenproof dish. Mix remaining cheese and grissini crumbs together and sprinkle over each one. Cook in the oven for 25 minutes, until golden brown. Top with thick sour cream and garnish with thyme, and chillies if desired.

Serves 4.

Red Cabbage & Sausage Braise

500 g (1 lb) red cabbage
90 g (3 oz) butter
1 large Spanish onion, chopped
1 clove garlic, crushed
2 tablespoons light soft brown sugar
2 tablespoons cider or wine vinegar
315 ml (10 fl oz/1¼ cups) chicken stock
salt and pepper, to taste
¼-½ teaspoon caraway seeds (optional)
4 frankfurters
125 g (4 oz) each Chorizo and Zywiecka sausage
1 large cooking apple
750 g (1½ lb) potatoes, cut into even pieces
TO GARNISH:
watercress sprigs
apple slices

1 Preheat oven to 150C (300F/Gas 2). Cut cabbage into quarters, discarding stalk; shred finely. Heat 60 g (2 oz) butter in a flameproof, enamel-lined casserole. Add onion, garlic and sugar and cook gently for 5 minutes. Add cabbage and cook for 5 minutes, stirring. Add vinegar, stock, seasoning, and caraway seeds, if desired. Stir well, cover and cook in oven for 1¼ hours.

2 Meanwhile, cut frankfurters, Chorizo and Zywiecka sausages into chunky slices. Peel, core and chop apple. Add sausages and apple to casserole, stir well; cover and cook for 30 minutes.

3 Meanwhile, cook potatoes in boiling salted water for 15-20 minutes, until tender. Drain, return to pan and place over a low heat for a few seconds to dry off. Mash with remaining butter and seasoning; beat until smooth. Transfer to a piping bag fitted with a large star nozzle and pipe borders around the edge of 4 individual serving dishes. Spoon cabbage mixture into centre. Garnish with watercress and apple to serve.

Serves 4.

Note: Zwyiecka is a smoked garlic spiced sausage available from delicatessens and good supermarkets.

Fennel Italiano

4 large fennel bulbs
2 tablespoons olive oil
2 cloves garlic, chopped
1 large onion, quartered and thinly sliced
397 g (14 oz) can peeled tomatoes, chopped
2 tablespoons tomato purée (paste)
90 ml (3 fl oz/⅓ cup) dry white wine or dry
vermouth
salt and pepper, to taste
185 g (6 oz) mozzarella cheese, thinly sliced
2-3 teaspoons chopped marjoram
TO GARNISH:
black olives

1 Preheat oven to 180C (350F/Gas 4). Cut off and reserve fennel fronds for garnishing. Cut fennel bulbs into quarters. Cook in boiling salted water to cover for 15 minutes; drain well.

2 Meanwhile in a pan, heat oil, add garlic and onion and fry gently for 5 minutes. Add tomatoes with their juice, tomato purée (paste) and wine or vermouth. Season with salt and pepper. Bring to the boil, then simmer, uncovered, for 10 minutes. Transfer to a blender or food processor; work until smooth.

3 Arrange fennel in 4 greased individual ovenproof dishes. Pour over sauce and cover with mozzarella cheese. Sprinkle with marjoram and freshly ground pepper. Cook in the oven for 30-40 minutes or until fennel is tender. Garnish with olives and reserved fennel fronds. Serve hot, with warm crusty bread.

Serves 4.

Gruyère & Tomato Jalousie

1 tablespoon olive oil
2 courgettes (zucchini), chopped
1 small onion, chopped
125 g (4 oz) beefsteak tomato, chopped
2 teaspoons chopped oregano
1 clove garlic, crushed
salt and pepper, to taste
60 g (2 oz/½ cup) grated Gruyère cheese
30 g (1 oz) unsalted cashews, ground
397 g (14 oz) packet puff pastry, thawed if frozen
beaten egg, to glaze
TO GARNISH:
sprigs of oregano

1 In a saucepan, heat oil, add courgettes (zucchini) and onion and fry for 3 minutes. Remove from heat, add tomato, oregano, garlic and seasoning. Cool in a strainer, then stir in cheese and ground nuts.

2 On a lightly floured surface, roll out pastry thinly to a 30.5 cm (12 in) square. Mark into two pieces, one 30.5 × 16 cm (12 × 6½ in) and the other 30.5 × 14 cm (12 × 5½ in). Put the smaller piece on a dampened baking sheet; cover with courgette (zucchini) mixture to within 1 cm (½ in) of edges. Brush border with beaten egg.

Sprinkle other pastry lightly with flour, then fold in half lengthwise. Lightly mark a margin about 2 cm (¾ in) from the three cut edges. Using a sharp knife, cut into the folded edge at 5 mm (¼ in) intervals within the marked margin.

3 Lift pastry over half the filling; unfold to cover remaining area. Seal edges, then knock up and flute. Chill for 30 minutes. Preheat oven to 220C (425F/Gas 7).

Brush jalousie lightly with beaten egg. Cook in the oven for 15 minutes. Reduce heat to 190C (375F/Gas 5) and cook for a further 15 minutes, until golden. Serve hot or cold, garnished with oregano.

Serves 4-6.

Ratatouille Cheese Gougère

CHOUX PASTRY:
52 g (1¾ oz) butter
75 g (2½ oz/⅔ cup) plain flour, sifted
2 eggs, beaten
60 g (2 oz) Lancashire cheese, crumbled
FILLING:
1 aubergine (eggplant)
1 large courgette (zucchini)
salt
3 tablespoons olive oil
2 red peppers, cored, seeded and cut into 2.5 cm
(1 in) pieces
1 Spanish onion, quartered and sliced
1 clove garlic, crushed
1 large tomato, skinned and chopped
salt and pepper, to taste

1 First, prepare filling: quarter aubergine (eggplant); cut aubergine (eggplant) quarters and courgette (zucchini) into 5 mm (¼ in) slices. Arrange in a colander, sprinkling each layer with salt. Leave for 30 minutes.

2 Preheat oven to 200C (400F/Gas 6). To make pastry, in a saucepan, put butter and 155 ml (5 fl oz/⅔ cup) water; heat gently until butter has melted. Bring to the boil, remove from heat and immediately add flour, all at once, with a pinch of salt, stirring quickly with a wooden spoon until smooth. Return pan to heat for a few seconds and beat until mixture forms a ball and leaves side of pan clean. Remove from heat and gradually add eggs, beating after each addition until glossy. Stir in cheese. Spoon mixture around edge of 4 greased individual ovenproof dishes. Cook in the oven for 30 minutes, or until well risen and golden.

3 Meanwhile, rinse aubergine (eggplant) and courgette (zucchini); drain and pat dry. In a pan, heat oil, add all filling ingredients, cover and cook gently for 30 minutes. Turn ratatouille into the centre of the choux rings and serve immediately.

Serves 4.

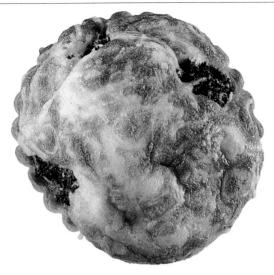

Broccoli Soufflé Tartlets

PASTRY:
185 g (6 oz/1½ cups) plain flour, sifted
60 g (2 oz/½ cup) wholemeal flour
pinch of salt
60 g (2 oz) block margarine, diced
60 g (2 oz) white vegetable fat, diced
155 g (5 oz/1¼ cups) finely grated Cheddar cheese
FILLING AND TOPPING:
375 g (12 oz) broccoli spears, cut into even-sized
spears
60 g (2 oz) butter
45 g (1½ oz/just over ¼ cup) plain flour
315 ml (10 fl oz/1¼ cups) milk
2 eggs, separated
salt and pepper, to taste

1 Preheat oven to 200C (400F/Gas 6). To make pastry, put flours and salt in a bowl and rub in fats. Add 60 g (2 oz/½ cup) cheese and mix well. Stir in 3-4 tablespoons cold water and mix to a firm dough. Knead gently and divide into 6 pieces. On a lightly floured surface, roll out and use to line six 11 cm (4 in) diameter, 2 cm (¾ in) deep, fluted flan tins. Prick bases with a fork. Line with foil and fill with baking beans. Cook for 5 minutes; remove foil and beans and cook for a further 5 minutes. Reduce heat to 190C (375F/Gas 5).

2 Cook broccoli in boiling salted water for 6-8 minutes. Drain and cut into pieces. In a pan, melt butter, stir in flour and cook for 1 minute. Blend in milk, bring to boil, stirring. Cook for 2 minutes.

3 Arrange half the broccoli in tartlet cases. In a blender or food processor, blend remaining broccoli with sauce, egg yolks and 60 g (2 oz/½ cup) remaining cheese. Season and transfer to a bowl. Whisk egg whites stiffly, then lightly fold into sauce. Spoon over broccoli in tartlet cases and sprinkle with remaining cheese. Cook in the oven for 20 minutes, until golden. Serve hot.

Serves 6.

Spinach & Ricotta Roulade

750 g (1½ lb) spinach
30 g (1 oz) butter
3 shallots, very finely chopped
45 g (1½ oz/⅓ cup) plain flour
155 ml (5 fl oz/⅔ cup) milk
15 g (½ oz/6 teaspoons) grated Parmesan cheese
4 large eggs, separated
salt and pepper, to taste
FILLING:
2 tablespoons thick sour cream
250 g (8 oz) ricotta cheese
3 spring onions, chopped
2 tablespoons chopped parsley
2-3 pinches cayenne pepper
TO GARNISH:
radish roses (prepared as tomato roses, page 115)

1 Lightly grease a 23 × 36 cm (9 × 14 in) Swiss roll tin and line with lightly greased non-stick paper. Preheat oven to 200C (400F/Gas 6).

Prepare and cook spinach (as for Spinach & Anchovy Soufflé, page 86). In a saucepan, melt butter, add shallots and fry gently for 3 minutes. Stir in flour and cook for 1 minute, then gradually blend in milk. Bring to the boil, then cook for 2 minutes, stirring. (The sauce will be very thick.) Remove from heat and stir in spinach, Parmesan cheese and egg yolks. Add salt and pepper and beat well.

2 Whisk egg whites until stiff but not dry; using a metal spoon, lightly fold into mixture. Spread into prepared tin, level surface and cook in the oven for 25 minutes or until set and firm to the touch.

Meanwhile, in a bowl, mix together filling ingredients; season with salt.

3 Turn roulade onto a sheet of lightly greased, non-stick paper. Loosen edges from lining paper and remove it in strips. Spread roulade with filling. Roll up, starting from a short side and using paper to help. Serve hot, garnished with radish roses.

Serves 6.

Sorrel & Asparagus Crêpes

24 young tender sorrel leaves
¼ bunch watercress
60 g (2 oz) unsalted butter
155 g (5 oz/1¼ cups) plain flour
pinch of salt
2 eggs, beaten
250 ml (8 fl oz/1 cup) milk
1-2 tablespoons corn oil
500 g (1 lb) asparagus spears
2 tablespoons lemon juice
185 ml (6 fl oz/¾ cup) Greek yogurt
salt and pepper, to taste
2 tomatoes, sliced
60 g (2 oz/½ cup) grated Emmenthal cheese
TO GARNISH:
lemon wedges

1 Shred sorrel. Chop watercress. In a saucepan, melt 15 g (½ oz) butter, add sorrel and watercress; cook gently for 2 minutes; cool.

Sift flour and salt into a bowl. Add eggs and gradually beat in milk and 155 ml (5 fl oz/⅔ cup) water. Stir in sorrel and watercress; transfer to a jug.

2 In a 17.5-20 cm (7-8 in) frying pan, heat a little oil, swirling it over base and side. Pour in enough batter to coat base of pan evenly. Cook over high heat for 2 minutes; turn and cook the other side until golden; set aside. Use remaining batter to make 7 more crêpes.

3 Preheat oven to 180C (350F/Gas 4). Prepare and cook asparagus (as for Parma & Asparagus Parcels, page 82); cut into bite-sized pieces. Melt remaining butter in a pan; remove from heat. Add lemon juice, yogurt and salt and pepper. Spoon over crêpes; fold each in half, then in half again. Insert asparagus into folds.

Arrange crêpes in a greased shallow ovenproof dish; put tomato slices between them and sprinkle with cheese. Cover with foil and cook in the oven for 15 minutes; uncover and cook for 7 minutes. Garnish with lemon wedges.

Serves 4.

Stir-fried Vegetable Nests

500 g (1 lb) potatoes
½ teaspoon salt
60 g (2 oz/½ cup) cornflour plus 2 teaspoons
vegetable oil for deep-frying
¼ Chinese cabbage
1 green pepper, cored and seeded
10 canned water chestnuts
5 sticks celery
3 carrots
1 fresh green chilli
3 tablespoons peanut oil
1 clove garlic, crushed
3 tablespoons Teriyaki sauce
2 tablespoons hoisin sauce

1 Finely grate potatoes into a colander; rinse well under cold running water; drain well and thoroughly pat dry on absorbent kitchen paper. Put into a bowl, add salt and 60 g (2 oz/½ cup) cornflour and mix well. Divide into 4 portions. Put one portion in an 11 cm (4 in) metal sieve (or game chip basket); spread out potato to cover inside of sieve evenly. Put a slightly smaller sieve inside (to keep shape during cooking).
2 Two-thirds fill a wok or deep pan with vegetable oil and heat to 180C (350F). Lower sieves into hot oil and fry for 4 minutes until potato is golden; drain. Carefully loosen potato nest and keep warm. Cook remaining 3 nests in the same way.
3 Shred cabbage. Dice pepper. Slice water chestnuts. Thinly slice celery. Peel and cut carrots into matchstick strips. Chop chilli, discarding seeds. In a wok or frying pan, heat peanut oil, add garlic and vegetables; stir-fry for 3 minutes.

Blend remaining cornflour with 4 tablespoons water, Teriyaki and hoisin sauces; add to pan and cook for 3 minutes, stirring. Spoon into potato nests. Serve hot.

Serves 4.

Scorzonera & Chicory au Gratin

250 g (8 oz) scorzonera
4 heads of chicory (Belgian endive)
1 teaspoon lemon juice
45 g (1½ oz) butter
3 tablespoons plain flour
155 ml (5 fl oz/⅔ cup) milk
½ teaspoon Dijon mustard
1-2 tablespoons chopped chervil
125 g (4 oz/1 cup) grated Gruyère or Emmenthal
cheese
salt and pepper, to taste
2 large slices cooked ham, halved
TO GARNISH:
3 small tomatoes
sprigs of chervil

 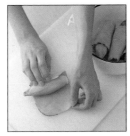 

1 Peel scorzonera and cut into 5 cm (2 in) pieces. Put in a saucepan with whole chicory (Belgian endive), lemon juice and boiling water to cover. Simmer, covered, for 10 minutes. Drain, reserving 250 ml (8 fl oz/1 cup) liquor; set aside.

2 Preheat oven to 200C (400F/Gas 6). In a pan, melt butter, stir in flour and cook for 1 minute. Blend in milk and reserved liquor; bring to the boil, stirring, then simmer for 2 minutes, stirring. Remove from heat, stir in mustard, chervil, half the cheese and salt and pepper.

Pat chicory (Belgian endive) dry with absorbent kitchen paper. Put scorzonera in 4 individual greased ovenproof dishes. Wrap chicory in ham and place on top. Pour over sauce and top with remaining cheese. Cook in oven for 25 minutes, until golden brown.

3 Make vandyke tomatoes for garnish. Insert a sharp pointed knife midway between stalk end and top of tomatoes; cut all the way round with a zig-zag motion, through to centre; separate halves. Garnish dish with tomatoes and chervil.

Serves 4.

Variation: Salsify may be used instead of scorzonera.

Artichokes Dauphinoise

750 g (1½ lb) Jerusalem artichokes
45 g (1½ oz) butter
1 clove garlic, crushed
salt and pepper, to taste
155 ml (5 fl oz/⅔ cup) single (light) cream
2 tablespoons milk
60 g (2 oz/½ cup) grated Gruyère cheese
a little freshly grated nutmeg
TO GARNISH:
sprigs of sage

1 Scrub artichokes well in cold water, but do not peel. Cook in boiling water to cover for 8-10 minutes, until par-cooked; drain well. Leave until cool enough to handle, then peel and cut into thin slices.

2 Preheat oven to 180C (350F/Gas 4). Mix butter with garlic and use half to grease a 23 cm (9 in) shallow ovenproof dish. Arrange one third of the artichoke slices over the base of the dish and season well with salt and pepper. Repeat layers, seasoning each layer.

3 Heat cream and milk in a small saucepan until hot, but not boiling. Pour over artichokes, sprinkle with cheese and nutmeg, and dot with remaining garlic-flavoured butter. Cook in the oven for 45 minutes, until golden brown. Serve hot, garnished with sage.

Serves 4.

Variation: Use new potatoes for this dish when artichokes are unavailable – cooked this way they are extremely good.

Glazed Vegetables with Madeira

6 courgettes (zucchini)
500 g (1 lb) maincrop carrots
vegetable oil for deep-frying
60 g (2 oz) unsalted butter
1 teaspoon green peppercorns, coarsely crushed
salt, to taste
finely grated rind and juice of 1 lime
2-3 teaspoons Madeira
TO GARNISH:
8 large sprigs of parsley
lime twists

1 Using a canelle knife, cut thin grooves down the length of the courgettes (zucchini); slice thinly; set aside. Peel carrots, slice thinly and cook in boiling salted water for 3 minutes. Drain, refresh with cold water and drain again; set aside.

Rinse and dry parsley for garnish thoroughly on absorbent kitchen paper.

Half-fill a deep pan with oil and preheat to 185C (365F), or until a cube of day-old bread browns in 45 seconds; turn off heat until ready to prepare garnish.

2 In a frying pan, melt butter, add courgettes (zucchini) and sauté for 1 minute. Add carrots and cook for 2 minutes, stirring frequently to glaze. Stir in crushed peppercorns, salt, lime rind and juice and heat through for 1 minute. Transfer to a warmed serving dish. Add Madeira to pan, deglaze and pour over vegetables. Keep warm while preparing garnish.

3 Reheat oil for deep-frying to 185C (365F). Put parsley sprigs into frying basket and submerge into hot oil (take great care as the oil will sizzle and froth); cook for a few seconds until sizzling stops. Drain briefly. Garnish vegetables with parsley and lime twists.

Serves 4-6.

French-fried Celeriac

500 g (1 lb) celeriac
1 slice of lemon
2 egg whites
125 g (4 oz/2 cups) fresh white breadcrumbs
½ teaspoon dried mixed herbs
vegetable oil for deep-frying
CHILLI DIP:
2 tablespoons tomato purée (paste)
2 teaspoons chilli sauce
1 clove garlic, crushed
1 teaspoon sesame oil
6 tablespoons mayonnaise
1 teaspoon lemon juice
TO GARNISH:
flat-leaf parsley

1 Peel and cut celeriac into quarters, then slice into 5 mm (¼ in) slices. Put into a pan of boiling salted water, with a slice of lemon added, and cook for 5 minutes. Drain, return to pan and shake over low heat for a few seconds to dry off; cool.

2 To make chilli dip, in a saucepan, put tomato purée (paste), chilli sauce, garlic, sesame oil and 3 tablespoons water; simmer for 2 minutes. Cool, then mix with mayonnaise and lemon juice; transfer to a small serving bowl and chill until required.

3 In a bowl, lightly beat egg whites until broken up and slightly frothy.

On a plate, mix breadcrumbs with herbs. Dip slices of celeriac into egg white, allow excess to drain off, then coat in breadcrumb mixture, pressing on firmly with fingers. Half-fill a deep pan with oil and heat to 190C (375F), or until a cube of day-old bread browns in 40 seconds. Lower celeriac slices into hot oil, a few at a time, and deep-fry for about 3 minutes, until golden brown and crisp. Drain on absorbent kitchen paper and keep warm while frying remainder. Serve hot, garnished with parsley and accompanied by chilli dip.

Serves 4-6.

Spiced Broccoli & Cauliflower

250 g (8 oz) broccoli spears
½ cauliflower
4 cardamom pods
60 g (2 oz) butter
1 small onion, thinly sliced and separated into rings
½ teaspoon cumin seeds
¼ teaspoon ground coriander
1 cm (½ in) piece fresh root (green) ginger, peeled
and grated
¼-½ teaspoon turmeric
1 clove garlic, crushed (optional)
2 teaspoons lemon juice
salt, to taste
a little natural yogurt (optional)
TO GARNISH:
sprigs of coriander

1 Cut off broccoli flowerets and divide into even-sized pieces. Cut stalks in half lengthwise, then cut into neat bite-sized pieces. Divide cauliflower into even-sized flowerets, discarding centre stalk. Cook broccoli stalks in a little boiling salted water for 3 minutes. Add cauliflower and broccoli flowerets and continue cooking for 3 minutes, until vegetables are barely tender; drain well.

2 Meanwhile, crush cardamom pods and remove seeds. In a frying pan, melt butter, add onion, cumin seeds, coriander, ginger, cardamom, turmeric and garlic, if desired. Cook gently for 5 minutes, stirring frequently. Add lemon juice and cook for 3 minutes. Season with salt.

3 Add prepared broccoli and cauliflower to pan, toss gently in spiced butter and heat through for 3 minutes, stirring gently. Transfer to a warmed serving dish, drizzle with yogurt, if desired, and garnish with coriander.

Serves 4.

Fried Wild Rice & Vegetables

60 g (2 oz/⅓ cup) wild rice
125 g (4 oz /⅔ cup) Basmati rice
185 g (6 oz) beansprouts
2 eggs
salt and pepper, to taste
7 g (¼ oz) butter
6 tablespoons corn oil
2 sticks celery, thinly sliced diagonally
1 leek, finely shredded
1 clove garlic, crushed
1 teaspoon sesame oil
2-3 teaspoons sake or dry sherry
1-2 tablespoons light soy sauce
6 Webb's Wonderful or Cos (romaine) lettuce
leaves, shredded finely
celery leaves to garnish

1 Rinse wild and Basmati rice separately under cold running water. Cook wild rice in boiling salted water for 10 minutes. Add Basmati rice to pan and cook for 20 minutes. Rinse, drain and turn onto a plate. Cool, then chill for several hours or overnight.

Soak beansprouts in boiling water for 30 seconds; drain.

2 Beat eggs with 2 teaspoons water and seasoning. In an 18-20 cm (7-8 in) frying pan, heat butter, add egg and cook until underside is golden and top is set. Turn onto a flat surface; cool. Roll up, golden-side outside, and slice thinly; set aside.

In a wok or frying pan, heat 2 tablespoons corn oil, add celery, leek and garlic and stir-fry for 2 minutes. Add beansprouts and stir-fry for 1 minute. Add 2 tablespoons corn oil, stir in rice and fry, stirring for 2 minutes.

3 Add sesame oil, sake or sherry and seasoning and stir-fry for 2 minutes. Turn into a warmed serving dish; sprinkle with soy sauce. Heat remaining corn oil in pan, add lettuce and stir-fry for about 2 minutes, until slightly wilted and glistening. Arrange around rice. Garnish with omelette slices and celery leaves.

Serves 4.

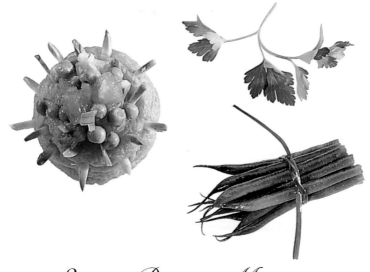

Sweet Potato Marquise

1 kg (2 lb) sweet potatoes, peeled
90 g (3 oz) butter
salt and pepper, to taste
2-3 pinches of ground mace
2 egg yolks
22 g (¾ oz) slivered almonds
125 g (4 oz) French beans
1 tablespoon corn oil
3 shallots, finely chopped
2 tomatoes, skinned and chopped
60 g (2 oz) frozen petits pois
4 tablespoons chicken stock
6-8 long chives
TO GARNISH:
sprigs of flat-leaf parsley

1 Cut sweet potatoes into even pieces and cook in boiling salted water for 15-20 minutes or until tender. Drain well, return to pan and shake over a low heat for a few seconds to dry off. Mash thoroughly. Add 60 g (2 oz) butter and season with salt, pepper and mace. Stir in egg yolks and beat well.

2 Preheat oven to 200C (400F/Gas 6). Lightly grease a baking sheet. Put potato mixture in a piping bag fitted with a 1 cm (½ in) plain nozzle and pipe 6-8 nests on the baking sheet. Melt remaining butter and brush lightly over nests; stud with almonds. Cook on top shelf of the oven for 15-20 minutes.

3 Meanwhile, trim beans, cut in half and cook in a steamer for 8-10 minutes or until tender.

Meanwhile, in a pan, heat oil. Add shallots, tomatoes, petits pois and stock, cover and cook gently for 5-6 minutes; season with salt and pepper and keep warm.

Divide steamed beans into 6-8 bundles and tie with chives.

Transfer sweet potato nests to a warmed serving plate and fill with petits pois mixture. Arrange bundles of beans attractively between nests. Garnish with parsley and serve hot.

Serves 6-8.

Jansson's Temptation

750 g (1½ lb) potatoes, peeled
60 g (2 oz) unsalted butter
1 large onion, quartered and thinly sliced
90 ml (3 fl oz/⅓ cup) double (thick) cream
125 ml (4 fl oz/½ cup) milk
50 g (2 oz) can anchovy fillets, drained
salt and pepper, to taste
6 tablespoons fresh white breadcrumbs
TO GARNISH:
sprigs of flat-leaf parsley

1 Preheat oven to 200C (400F/Gas 6). Cut potatoes in half lengthwise. Place flat-side down and cut into 3 mm (⅛ in) slices, then cut slices into 5 mm (¼ in) matchstick strips. In a large frying pan, melt 45 g (1½ oz) butter, add onion and fry gently for 5 minutes, stirring occasionally.

2 Add potato sticks and continue frying gently for 5 minutes, stirring frequently to prevent sticking. Remove from heat. Mix cream and milk together. Put half onion and potato mixture in a shallow ovenproof dish. Chop half the anchovies and sprinkle over top. Season lightly with salt and liberally with pepper. Pour over half the cream mixture. Cover with remaining onion and potato mixture and press down firmly with a fish slice. Season again.

3 Sprinkle breadcrumbs evenly over surface and press lightly. Pour over remaining cream mixture. Melt remaining butter and drizzle over top. Cook in the oven for 35-40 minutes, until golden brown and cooked through. Cut remaining anchovies in half lengthwise and arrange in a lattice design over the top. Garnish with parsley and serve hot.

Serves 4.

Garlic-baked Potatoes

750 g (1½ lb) small, even-sized new potatoes
1 tablespoon corn oil
15 g (½ oz) butter
1 clove garlic, crushed
salt and pepper, to taste
2 sprigs of mint
4 rashers smoked streaky bacon, rinds removed
4 spring onions
TO GARNISH:
sprigs of mint

1 Preheat oven to 180C (350F/Gas 4). Scrub potatoes well under cold water, but do not peel. Leave whole and pat dry on absorbent kitchen paper. Prick each potato twice with a fine skewer.

2 In a flameproof casserole, heat oil and butter, add potatoes and fry for 5 minutes to brown lightly, turning frequently. Stir in garlic and salt and pepper. Add mint, cover and cook in the oven for 20 minutes or until almost tender.

3 Cut bacon into thin strips. Slice spring onions diagonally into thin slivers. Remove mint from casserole and stir in bacon and spring onions. Cook, uncovered, for 10 minutes, until bacon is crisp and potatoes are tender. Turn into a warmed serving dish and garnish with mint.

Serves 4.

Variation: Use 3-4 shallots instead of spring onions; thinly slice and separate them into rings.

Antipasto Salad

500 g (1 lb) eddoes (taros)
2 tablespoons snipped chives
1 tablespoon chopped parsley
2 heads of red or white chicory
1 large fennel bulb
1 green pepper, cored and seeded
1 beefsteak tomato
½ head curly endive
½ ripe Ogen melon
DRESSING:
3 tablespoons walnut oil
3 tablespoons sunflower oil
2 tablespoons white wine vinegar or lemon juice
1 clove garlic, crushed
salt and pepper, to taste

1 Peel eddoes (taros), cut into even-sized pieces and cook in boiling salted water for 10-15 minutes, until just tender (take care not to overcook). Drain and leave until cool enough to handle, then dice and put in a bowl. In a small bowl, whisk the dressing ingredients together. Pour 4 tablespoons dressing over warm eddoes, add herbs and mix gently to avoid breaking up eddoes. Leave to cool.
2 Separate chicory into leaves. Cut fennel into quarters and separate into layers. Slice pepper into rings. Thinly slice tomato. Divide endive into leaves. Cut melon into thin slices, discard seeds, then cut flesh away from skin.
3 Arrange curly endive on individual serving platters. Spoon eddoe salad into the centre. Arrange other prepared vegetables and melon around eddoe. Whisk remaining dressing until thoroughly combined and drizzle over salad.

Serves 4-6.

Variation: Use new potatoes or par-cooked celeriac instead of eddoes.

Ribbon & Rose Salad

2 courgettes (zucchini)
2 large carrots
1 mooli (daikon)
DRESSING:
155 ml (5 fl oz/²⁄₃ cup) mayonnaise
2 tablespoons snipped chives
1 clove garlic, crushed
1 tablespoon lemon juice
1 teaspoon tomato purée (paste)
1 tablespoon single (light) cream
½ teaspoon caster sugar
salt and pepper, to taste
TO GARNISH:
12 small round radishes

1 Have ready a large bowl of cold water, filled with 24 ice cubes. Using a potato peeler, cut as many very thin lengthwise slices as possible from courgettes (zucchini). Drop into iced water. Peel carrots and mooli and repeat procedure.
2 To make radish roses for garnish, trim away root ends and larger leaves – leave on the smallest leaf as these look attractive. Using a small, sharp, pointed knife, cut 3 petals from root to leaf end of radish, taking care not to cut right through. Place in the iced water.

Push all vegetables down into water and leave in the refrigerator for several hours to crisp and slightly curl 'ribbons' and open out 'roses'.
3 To make the dressing, put all ingredients in a bowl and mix well. Transfer to 4 small dishes and place on individual serving plates.

Drain vegetables and pat dry. Arrange 'ribbons' of vegetables around the bowls of dressing and use the radish 'roses' to garnish each salad.

Serves 4.

Spinach & Bacon Salad

250 g (8 oz) tender, young spinach
8 rashers streaky bacon, rinds removed
2 slices white bread
2 shallots
125 ml (4 fl oz/½ cup) olive oil
1 clove garlic, crushed
60 g (2 oz/⅓ cup) seeded muscatel raisins, halved if large
2 egg yolks
½ teaspoon dry mustard
4 anchovy fillets, mashed finely
6 teaspoons lemon juice
6 teaspoons grated Parmesan cheese
1 teaspoon caster sugar
pepper, to taste

1 Remove stalks from rinsed and dried spinach. Tear leaves into bite-sized pieces, if necessary, and place in a serving bowl. Cut bacon into small pieces. Remove crusts and cut bread into neat cubes. Thinly slice shallots and separate into rings.
2 Dry-fry bacon in a non-stick frying pan, without additional fat, until crisp and golden. Drain and leave to cool. Mix oil with garlic and add 2 tablespoons to bacon fat in frying pan. Add bread cubes and fry until golden brown, turning frequently; drain and leave to cool.

Add bacon, raisins and shallots to spinach and mix lightly. Chill until required.
3 In a bowl, mix together egg yolks, mustard, anchovies, lemon juice, Parmesan and sugar. Season with pepper, then gradually whisk in remaining garlic-flavoured oil in a thin stream, whisking well to yield a smooth sauce. Just before serving, add dressing to salad and toss lightly until all ingredients are evenly coated. Scatter croûtons over salad and serve immediately.

Serves 4.

Chicken & Prawn Salad

250 g (8 oz) skinned chicken breast fillet
250 g (8 oz) peeled prawns, thawed if frozen
2 teaspoons sesame oil
1 clove garlic, crushed
2.5 cm (1 in) piece fresh root (green) ginger, peeled
and grated
3 tablespoons light soy sauce
4 small firm tomatoes
¼ head Chinese cabbage
125 g (4 oz) beansprouts
½ head lollo rosso
generous handful of corn salad or lamb's lettuce
1 bunch watercress
2 tablespoons corn or peanut oil
1 onion, quartered and cut into thin slivers
2 teaspoons caster sugar

1 Cut chicken into fine slivers and put into a bowl. Add prawns, then stir in sesame oil, garlic, ginger and soy sauce. Mix well and leave to marinate for 30 minutes.

2 Meanwhile, prepare tomato roses for garnish. Using a small sharp knife and starting at the smooth end of each tomato, remove skin in an even, continuous strip about 1 cm (½ in) wide. Start to curl skin from base end, with flesh side inside, to form a bud-shape, then continue winding skin round bud-shape to form a 'rose'. Cover loosely with plastic wrap and chill until required.

Finely shred Chinese cabbage.

Soak beansprouts in boiling water for 15 seconds. Drain and refresh with cold water; drain again. Shred lollo rosso. Put prepared vegetables in a bowl, add corn salad or lamb's lettuce and watercress, reserving a few sprigs for garnish. Toss well, then transfer salad to a shallow serving dish.

3 In a wok or frying pan, heat oil, add onion and stir-fry for 2 minutes. Add prawn mixture and stir-fry for 3-4 minutes. Stir in sugar. Spoon hot mixture over salad. Garnish with tomato roses and watercress. Serve immediately.

Serves 4.

Endive & Roquefort Salad

250 g (8 oz) French beans, trimmed
2 heads of chicory (Belgian endive) separated into leaves
½ head curly endive (frisée), torn in bite-sized pieces
60 g (2 oz) shelled pecans
1 green pepper, cored, seeded and sliced into rings
2 tomatoes, cut into wedges
150 g (5 oz) Roquefort cheese
ROQUEFORT DRESSING:
2 egg yolks
1 teaspoon caster sugar
½ teaspoon each salt and pepper
½ teaspoon Dijon mustard
2 tablespoons lemon juice or white wine vinegar
315 ml (10 fl oz/1¼ cups) olive oil
2 tablespoons single (light) cream
3 teaspoons snipped chives

1 Cook French beans in a little boiling salted water for 6-8 minutes, until just tender. Drain and refresh under running cold water; drain again. Arrange chicory (Belgian endive) in a border around a serving bowl. Fill centre with endive (frisée). Arrange nuts, pepper rings and tomato wedges on top, allowing endive (frisée) to show around edge as a border. Dice 90 g (3 oz) Roquefort cheese and place in the centre of salad. Cover with plastic wrap and chill.

2 To make dressing, put egg yolks in a bowl, add sugar, salt, pepper and mustard and blend well with a wire whisk. Gradually blend in lemon juice or vinegar. Stand bowl on a damp tea-towel to keep it steady. Start adding oil, drop by drop, beating well after each addition, until about a quarter has been added. Gradually increase the amount of oil being added to a thin steady stream and continue beating to a thick consistency.

3 Stir cream into dressing. Finely crumble in remaining Roquefort and beat until smooth. Stir in chives and transfer to a serving bowl. Serve with the salad.

Serves 4.

Italian Salad Cups

1 green pepper
16 cherry tomatoes, halved
8 stoned black olives
8 stuffed green olives
4 spring onions
125 g (4 oz) mozzarella cheese
1 radicchio
DRESSING:
3 tablespoons olive oil
1 tablespoon red wine vinegar
1 clove garlic, crushed
salt and pepper, to taste
½ teaspoon wholegrain mustard
½ teaspoon caster sugar
TO GARNISH:
sprigs of oregano

1 Skewer green pepper firmly on a fork and hold over a gas-flame until the skin blisters and blackens. Alternatively, cut green pepper in half and place, skin-side up, in a grill pan. Preheat grill to high and grill pepper until skin blisters and blackens. Allow to cool, then peel away skin. Discard stalk end, core and seeds; cut pepper into thin slivers and place in a bowl with the tomatoes.

2 Slice olives; thinly slice spring onions. Cut cheese into small cubes. Add olives, spring onions and cheese to bowl and toss gently.

Cut stem end off radicchio and carefully separate leaves. Select 8 cup-shaped leaves, rinse in cold water and pat dry. Wash and finely shred 4 more radicchio leaves and add to bowl.

3. Put all dressing ingredients in a screw-top jar and shake vigorously until well blended. Add to salad ingredients and toss together lightly. Fill radicchio cups with salad mixture and arrange on a serving plate. Garnish with oregano.

Serves 4, or 8 as a starter.

Lettuce & Avocado Salad

2 Little Gem lettuce
1 large ripe avocado
1 teaspoon lemon juice
DRESSING:
125 g (4 oz) raspberries
2 teaspoons caster sugar
5 teaspoons distilled malt vinegar
3 tablespoons sunflower oil
salt and pepper, to taste
TO GARNISH:
chives

1 First prepare dressing: put 90 g (3 oz) raspberries in a bowl; add sugar. Set aside remaining raspberries for garnish. Heat vinegar in a small saucepan until hot; pour over raspberries and leave to cool. Strain through a fine nylon sieve into a bowl, pressing raspberries with the back of a wooden spoon to extract all the juice and flesh. Add oil to raspberry mixture in bowl and season with salt and pepper. Whisk together until blended.

2 Cut lettuce neatly into quarters and arrange on a serving platter. Halve avocado, remove stone and peel away skin; cut flesh neatly lengthwise into slices and brush with lemon juice.

3 Arrange avocado slices and lettuce on individual serving dishes. Just before serving, whisk dressing again and spoon a little over salad. Serve remainder separately. Garnish salad with remaining raspberries and chives.

Serves 4.

Cucumber & Strawberry Salad

16 mange tout (snow peas)
½ cucumber
12 large strawberries
DRESSING:
3 tablespoons sunflower oil
1 tablespoon white wine vinegar
½ teaspoon caster sugar
salt and pepper, to taste
2 teaspoons finely chopped mint
TO GARNISH:
6 sprigs of mint
a little beaten egg white
a little caster sugar

1 First prepare mint sprigs for garnish. Gently rinse mint sprigs and pat dry. Brush lightly with beaten egg white, then coat with caster sugar, shaking off excess. Leave on greaseproof paper for at least 1 hour to dry. Trim mange tout (snow peas) and blanch in boiling water for 1 minute. Drain, refresh in cold water; drain and pat dry. Set aside.
2 Using the notch of a canelle knife, remove lengthwise strips of skin from cucumber at regular intervals; slice cucumber thinly. Cut strawberries into thin slices.
3 Arrange mange tout (snow peas) in a border on individual serving plates. Arrange cucumber slices in overlapping circles inside. Arrange strawberries in centre. Put dressing ingredients in a screw-top jar and shake vigorously until well blended. Spoon over salad just before serving. Garnish with frosted mint sprigs.

Serves 4.

Variation: Omit dressing and serve salad with a little chilled white or rosé wine spooned over just before serving.